A Year of Cats...In Hats!

CRAFTS TO MAKE YOU SMILE

Sheila Haynes Raven

Martingale®
& COMPANY

◎ Dedication ◎

To the memory of women across the ages who have "made do" with whatever materials they had at hand to bring beauty and comfort to their families. Whether sewing, cooking, gardening, or tending home, they were demonstrating their love and creativity. May we be inspired by their devotion and carry on in our own ways, passing on what we know to future generations.

◎ Acknowledgments ◎

I am grateful to those quilters and artists who have paved the way for our generation. I feel such a strong connection with them and I'm constantly inspired as I study more and more about their individual journeys.

Thanks to my wonderful friends in the Smoky Mountain Quilt Guild, especially the girls at Thursday Bee. Girlfriends are essential, and the ladies of Thursday Bee are supreme. They are the most supportive and inspiring group you can imagine.

Thanks to the many people I have met or have written to me saying that they were inspired by my work. You never cease to inspire me and I hope each and every one of you will pursue your creative dreams. Be fearless!

Thanks to the people at Martingale & Company for signing on for another book from me. Writing my first book, *Sassy Cats: Purr-fect Craft Projects,* was such a joy, and I knew that there were additional books in my head. A special thanks to Mary Green and Dawn Anderson for their encouragement and support.

I'm grateful to my wonderful family, especially Larry and our girls, Haverly and Julie. They've been very patient and supportive when I was knee-deep in deadlines.

Thanks to the many people in the arts and crafts industry for their goodwill and support, especially Carol Duvall; David Peha of Clothworks Fabrics; Bernina USA; Sulky of America; YLI; Jacquard Products; National Nonwovens; Delta Technical Coatings, Inc.; Loew-Cornell; Fiskars; and the Warm Company.

A Year of Cats . . . in Hats!
Crafts to Make You Smile
© 2004 by Sheila Haynes Rauen

Martingale & Company
20205 144th Avenue NE
Woodinville, WA 98072-8478
www.martingale-pub.com

Printed in China
09 08 07 06 05 04   8 7 6 5 4 3 2 1

Library of Congress Cataloging-in-Publication Data

Rauen, Sheila Haynes.
　A year of cats—in hats! : crafts to make you smile / Sheila Haynes Rauen.
　　p. cm.
　ISBN 1-56477-529-1
　1. Handicraft. 2. Cats in art. 3. Quilting—Patterns. I. Title.
　TT157 .R375 2004
　745.5—dc22

　　　　　　　　　　　　　　　　　　2003021714

◎ Mission Statement ◎

Dedicated to providing quality products and service to inspire creativity.

◎ Credits ◎

President: Nancy J. Martin
CEO: Daniel J. Martin
Publisher: Jane Hamada
Editorial Director: Mary V. Green
Managing Editor: Tina Cook
Technical Editor: Karen Costello Soltys
Copy Editor: Liz McGehee
Design Director: Stan Green
Illustrator: Laurel Strand
Cover and Text Designer: Regina Girard
Photographer: Brent Kane

Contents

To say that I feel blessed to be doing the things I do is an understatement. I often look up from my work in the studio and say a prayer of thanks. Though it is a bit cluttered with all kinds of fabrics, paints, books, and CDs—as well as a treadmill—it's my little piece of heaven.

It's wonderful to be able to share my ideas and techniques with so many people by writing books. The seeds for this book were sown shortly after the publication of my first book, *Sassy Cats: Purr-fect Craft Projects.* I was in the studio when my Persian cat, Gabriel, came in to assist me. As I looked at him, it occurred to me that if cats wore hats, they would need two—one for each ear. The first manifestation of this idea took the form of a wall quilt, featuring five cats celebrating different holidays. Making this quilt was a wonderful learning experience for me and it helped hone my free-motion embroidery skills. This led to designing hats for cats for every month. Read on to see what I came up with for the 12 months of the year. I hope you enjoy the designs and will be inspired to experiment with different materials to create your own cats in hats!

This "Hairy Holidays" quilt inspired the idea for A Year of Cats . . . in Hats.

Preface

Though most of my artwork created for galleries is considered fiber art, I admit I love to work in a wide variety of media. In the past, people would say to me that I should focus on one thing. Being a bit of a rebel, I continued to experiment with different media, and my decision to do so has served me very well. In *A Year of Cats . . . in Hats!* you will find a variety of ways to use the designs for each month of the year. For those of you interested in quilting, you may choose to make all 12 of the designs and stitch them together with sashing to create a quilt. Another option is to make a wall hanging that includes the designs for each birthday month in your family. I have made each block individually and stitched small curtain rings to the back of each one. That way, you can hang a block on a painted wooden plaque (directions for painting the plaque are also included) and change the display each month.

The design area of the blocks is 8" square. With ½" binding around the blocks, the finished size is 9" square. You may prefer to work in a larger or smaller format. The designs can easily be reduced or enlarged to suit your needs.

Celebrate each month with a festive little quilt.

In addition to the quilt blocks, the book contains nine companion projects. I hope that they will inspire you to try different techniques. They demonstrate how versatile the designs can be with a little extra imagination. For instance, I reduced the February design slightly and painted it onto a heart-shaped papier-mâché box. The April design is a "purrfect" fit as an embellishment on an umbrella—you can

Chase away April showers with a hand-painted umbrella.

be sure no one else will have one like it. The May design has two companion projects: a painted glass vase and a table runner. I enlarged the August design and added two more fish to the design to create a floorcloth. I also love to work with felt and I have used it to make a purse or candy tote from the October design. The January and December designs are re-created in painted glass for holiday tree ornaments or for light catchers you can hang in a window.

Painted glass ornaments can double as sun catchers.

Introduction

I grew up in Tennessee in an old-fashioned extended family. Our grandparents lived at the top of the "Hill," and several aunts, uncles, and cousins lived scattered throughout the neighborhood. We had a very close family with three primary matriarchs, including my mom and her two sisters. We never met our grandmother on that side of the family, but we heard so many wonderful stories about her. She has been an influence on me just through these stories. She learned to quilt from her mother, my great-grandmother, Martha Jane Childress Moore. One of our favorite family photos shows five generations, including Martha Jane and her father, Calvin Lindsey Childress, who was a blacksmith and shoemaker during the Civil War. Stories passed down by family members tell how he would hide his tools when Confederate soldiers were reported to be in the area.

My grandmother, Nettie Lee White, daughter of Martha Jane, loved to make quilts. She would dream of a new design and sketch it out the next morning before it slipped from her mind. She was working on an English paper-piecing project at the time of her death in a car accident in the late 1930s. Unfortunately, none of her finished quilts have survived.

My grandparents, Audley David and Nettie Lee White, daughter of Martha Jane Childress Moore.

Five generations of my family taken sometime in the 1920s. Martha Jane Childress Moore on the left made the beautiful appliquéd quilt her father, Calvin Childress, is sitting on. The lady on the right is Martha Jane's daughter, Elthea. Elthea's daughter and grandson are pictured in the center.

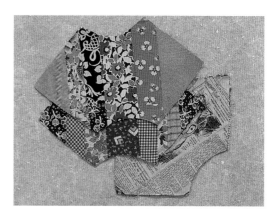

These quilt patches were made by my grandmother, Nettie Lee White, in the late 1930s. It's interesting to read the newspaper that she used as a foundation backing for stitching her fabrics.

Background and Inspiration

Although I didn't realize it earlier in my life, I can see where I got my creative genes. My mother was very artistic and encouraged us to draw and make things. One of my favorite things was a large blackboard she bought for us. Inspired by the many Western television shows at that time, I drew an elaborate battle scene. My mom bragged about it so much and took a photo to commemorate the event. She said that I was so proud of it that I drew it over and over again.

A colored-pencil portrait I did of three cats.

Me at about age six in front of one of my first masterpieces.

Another favorite topic for my early art work was Halloween. This particular piece may have foretold my later obsession with drawing and painting cats.

I drew this picture at about age six. Even then, cats were an important element of my artwork!

The matriarchs in the family were eventually joined by a wonderful new neighbor, Wray Stevens. She and her art-professor husband, Walter, along with their two children moved into the neighborhood and quickly became a part of our extended family. I was so impressed by the artistic talents of both Walter and Wray. He was a painter who spent most of his time in his studio. She created wonderful original pieces in fabrics and felt. Many of the children in our family are blessed with handmade soft-sculpture felt Christmas ornaments made by Wray during summers on the coast of Maine. She very patiently taught us some of the simple stitches and generously shared some of her patterns and materials.

For years, the ladies in my family would get together for coffee, conversation, and sometimes stitching once or twice a week on Friday and Saturday evenings. They provided a real training ground for me and my siblings. We learned so much from these sessions and benefited greatly from the support and encouragement of so many adults, including the men who sometimes joined us.

When I first started college, I planned to major in education and become a teacher. I really wanted to study art, but I had the misconception that you had to be very experienced to choose that path. Later on, I finally got the courage to switch my major to art and was thrilled from the first day in art class. I felt challenged, yet right at home at the same time. I soaked up drawing, painting, and art history like a sponge.

After I married, I spent many years being a stay-at-home mom as well as working on my undergraduate and graduate degrees. When our youngest was in kindergarten, I returned to school to get my master's degree and teaching credentials. After teaching high school art for a year, I realized more than ever that I wanted to be a full-time artist, but I wasn't sure how to do this.

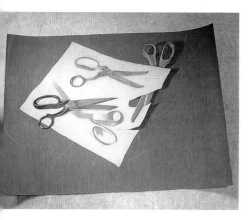

Prismacolor pencil drawing of a still life arrangement of scissors with photocopied image of the same scissors.

I went to work part-time at an art-supply store in our area. There I met many artists and designers who were pursuing their dreams. I had the freedom to experiment with different materials and often made creative displays to showcase the products in the store. One of the displays won the top regional award from an arts manufacturer. I did everything from paper sculpture to

Portrait of a dearly departed pet painted on silk, with a painted wooden frame.

designing and painting seasonal pieces. It was then that I decided to try my hand at silk painting. The manager encouraged me to display my work in the store, and it gained the attention of a computer mouse-pad manufacturer. This was my first licensing endeavor, and the pads were sold all over the country at bookstores and gift shops. The company that manufactured the paints I used for the silk paintings learned of my work and hired me as a freelance designer and spokesperson for their wide range of paints.

The company then started sending me to different trade shows to demonstrate their products, and I began making appearances on TV shows, such as the *Carol Duvall Show, Home Matters,* and *Simply Quilts.* I also started designing projects for magazines, such as *Family Circle* and *Woman's Day.* I've designed projects for everything from fabric painting and glass painting to home-decorating sewing projects.

Eventually, I quit working to devote myself full-time to art and design. I began to explore the use of quilting with silk painting. My love of sewing was resurfacing and I got more excited about the idea of incorporating different mediums in my work.

Since then, I have become more involved in the quilt world. I've attended many of the International Quilt Markets and this has helped me focus on the

Carol Duvall and me. Carol is holding a wall quilt I made that portrays her surrounded by assorted craft supplies. It was presented to her live on her show as a surprise.

paths I want to pursue. It led to the licensing of my art-work for use on fabric. Samples from my first line, called Bloomin' Birds, from Clothworks Fabrics in Seattle, Washington, can be seen in the table-runner project on page 51. I've fallen in love with painting on paper all over again, because to design the fabrics, I paint the designs on watercolor paper, using gouache paints.

Ideas for my work come at any time of the day or night. I choose to focus on whimsical subjects and often a title or phrase will come to me before the actual image does. In addition to studying art books for inspiration, I also find children's books to be a huge source of ideas.

Keeping a sketchbook and journal is an essential part of what I do. I would be lost without it. I highly recommend that you keep one as well. It will help you stay on track and focus on the priorities in your life,

no matter what you do. Whether you have an art background or you've never taken an art class in your life, I think you'll find it worthwhile to jot down your thoughts and ideas. You never know what wonderful projects can come of them!

I hope you will be inspired to create your own unique cats and hats. Whether you are a quilter, painter, or all-around crafter, I invite you to experiment with different mediums. Don't be afraid to break the rules and work outside your comfort zone. This is the best way to learn new approaches and bring freshness to your work. And besides, even if you've never tried working with a particular medium, you'll find a complete supplies list, step-by-step instructions, and color photographs of the completed projects to guide you along the way. You may just find you have a love for a new craft.

Swatches of the Bloomin' Birds fabric collection I designed for Clothworks.

Working with fabric provides endless possibilities. So many techniques and products make it fun to create your own unique projects. I used appliqué, quilting, hand and machine embroidery, fabric painting, stamping, and beading to create the quilt blocks and other fabric projects in *A Year of Cats . . . in Hats.*

Fusible Appliqué

You have many choices when it comes to appliqué, including hand and machine methods. If you prefer hand appliqué (needle-turn or freezer-paper method), you'll need to add a seam allowance to the designs in the book. Personally, I enjoy doing fusible appliqué, especially since I do so much embellishment work on top of the appliqué fabrics.

Fabric Techniques

For fusible appliqué, choose a fusible web or interfacing that will not gum up your needle. Products listed as "lightweight" or "sewable" are your best bets. Heavy-duty fusible web will very likely stick to your machine needle. Another factor is the weight of the fusible. I don't really worry about this too much since I don't make bed or snuggle quilts. In fact, one of my friends remarked one day that my art quilts would hold up like a tank. They do tend to be thick with layers. If you want to make bed quilts or baby quilts, choose fabrics and a fusible with softness in mind. You should also check to see if the fusible product is machine-washable or dry-cleanable. (For cotton appliqué, you'd want washable fusible web, but if you're working with silk, you may also want to make sure it can be dry-cleaned.)

I like to use Steam-A-Seam 2 fusible web for my appliqué. It is tacky on both sides and has paper layers on each side. I try to keep large quantities on hand. Or you may want to try Lite Steam-A-Seam 2 Double Stick for more delicate projects. It is best to store both products both in such a way that the paper sides remain in contact with the fusible layer. I keep mine in a plastic bag so they are not affected by humidity, which can release the paper backing from the web.

1. To use Steam-A-Seam 2, draw the desired shape in reverse onto either side of the Steam-A-Seam 2 and then cut around the shape, leaving a ¼" to ½" allowance around the marked line.

2. Remove the paper backing on the opposite side (without the drawn image) and hand press the fusible onto the back of your desired fabric. Cut the fusible and fabric along the drawn lines. It is now ready to be positioned on the background fabric. Repeat the process until all of the shapes are prepared.

3. Make a positioning guide or overlay before fusing the shapes in place. Tracing paper works pretty well, but I prefer acetate sheets (available at office-supply stores). Simply trace the entire design onto the tracing paper or acetate with a fine-point permanent pen, such as a Sharpie or Micron Pigma pen.

The overlay can be pinned into position over the background fabric, if you have a portable ironing pad. An alternative setup is to tape the overlay in place over the background fabric on a table or work surface.

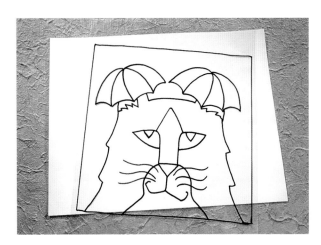

Block design traced onto transparent acetate is a good tool for positioning appliqués.

4. Working from back to front, position each shape, overlapping where indicated. With Steam-A-Seam 2, the tacky surface will hold the shapes in place until you're ready to iron them onto the background. You can reposition the pieces repeatedly until you're satisfied with the layout. With other fusible webs, you may want to pin them in place until you're finished with your layout.

5. Fuse the fabrics in place, following the manufacturer's directions.

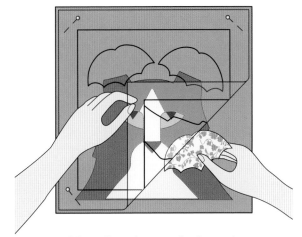

Slide appliqué shapes under the overlay to place them on the background.

Stabilizing

After all shapes are ironed in place, the entire piece should be stabilized before sewing. There are many ways to stabilize. Some people use fusible interfacing, and there are many products available for this purpose. I have several friends who use such things as freezer paper ironed onto the back of the fabric or regular computer paper or typing paper pinned in place.

One of my favorite stabilizers is Sulky's Totally Stable. It is an iron-on, tear-away stabilizer that is available in black and white and sold by the yard or as pre-packaged sheets. It is very easy to use and tears away effortlessly. It leaves no residue on the fabric. Iron it onto the back of the fabric, following the manufacturer's directions. It can be ironed on in sections if the area is too large for one piece. When working with larger appliqué pieces, it's also a good idea to use a few pins to help hold the stabilizer in place.

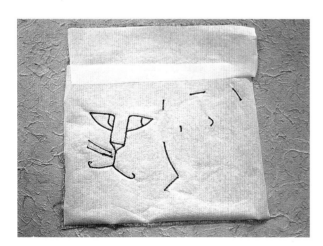

Wrong side of appliqué block with satin stitching showing on the stabilizer.

Stitching

Once the appliqué block or quilt top is stabilized, it's time to stitch the shapes into place. Decide whether you want to use a thread color to match each shape or if you would prefer to create more contrast by using different colors. I don't usually make all of these decisions up front. Appliqué is an ongoing, creative process, so I often change my mind as the piece develops. I prefer to use decorative threads, such as rayon embroidery threads, for appliqué rather than cotton or other sewing threads. I recommend using good quality threads such as those from Sulky, YLI, Isacord, and Superior Threads. I love the look of the metallic and holographic threads, too. I also use special bobbin thread. Lightweight bobbin thread comes in black or white and works well for most projects. If you are stitching a piece that will be seen from the front and the back, you may decide to use the same thread in the bobbin as in the needle.

Thread choices are numerous when it comes to machine appliqué. Rayon threads give a nice sheen, while metallic threads add some glitz.

An open-toe presser foot is your best choice for machine appliqué. It enables you to see your work more easily than with other presser feet because there is no metal or plastic bar across the front of your stitching area. Set your machine in the automatic needle-down position if it has this feature.

It is important to use the best-quality needles. I use needles made specifically for my machine by its manufacturer as well as other top-quality embroidery, metallic, and topstitching needles. I've been told that needles work most efficiently for about eight hours. I don't really time them, but I can tell when they have passed their prime. Your machine will tell you when the stitching doesn't seem quite right. Once the thread starts breaking, you're way overdue for a needle change.

It is also extremely important to keep your machine clean and well oiled; I cannot stress this enough. I don't recommend using canned air. I clean the bobbin area and the throat plate area after each project. I also oil the machine after cleaning. Periodically, I use my vacuum cleaner attachment to remove dust and fibers and to clean the area around the machine. Be sure to move any small objects around the machine before doing this.

I enjoy using the satin stitch (zigzag) or the blanket stitch on my machine to outline and appliqué the shapes. The feather stitch is another popular decorative stitch found on most newer machines.

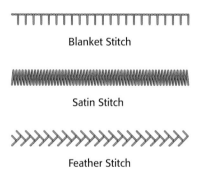

Blanket Stitch

Satin Stitch

Feather Stitch

There are times when I do not stitch around the edges of all the appliqués, mainly when I plan to do heavy free-motion embroidery work instead. An example of this type of stitching can be seen on the trees in the background of the Cold as Mice block on page 26. This was a design decision, with the goal being to create texture instead of a crisp line. I also did this on the trees for the Windy Kitty block on page 36. In addition to texture, I wanted to accentuate the feeling of the wind blowing. I often use this technique to create the texture of fur or feathers in my cats and other animals.

When appliquéing by machine, position your work under the presser foot so that the left swing position of the needle stitches into the appliqué, and the right swing position stitches into the background fabric just at the edge of the appliqué piece.

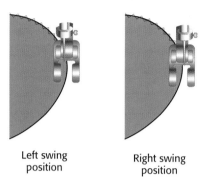

Left swing position   Right swing position

When stitching around curves, keep the needle in the fabric and lift the presser foot to turn the fabric slightly after every few stitches. To turn corners, leave the needle in the left swing position so that it is in the appliqué, lift the presser foot, turn the fabric, reposition the needle, and lower the presser foot so that you are ready to start sewing the next side of the appliqué piece.

After completing the stitching, tear away the stabilizer before proceeding to the next steps. One gadget that a lot of quilters find handy for paper removal is a hemostat. Using it to help remove the stabilizer makes the job so much easier. I recently discovered the many virtues of having hemostats (in two sizes) to help with various sewing and crafts tasks. My friend Elle Colquit of the Picket Fence recommended that I try them. She sells them on her Web site (see "Resources" on page 94). You can also find hemostats at many pharmacies or medical-supply companies.

Hand Appliqué and Embroidery

If preferred, you can appliqué any of the projects by hand. Just remember to add a ¼" seam allowance to the patterns before cutting them out. Techniques such as needle-turn and freezer-paper appliqué are popular alternatives to fusible appliqué. There are several hand embroidery stitches suited to stitching and embellishing hand appliqué.

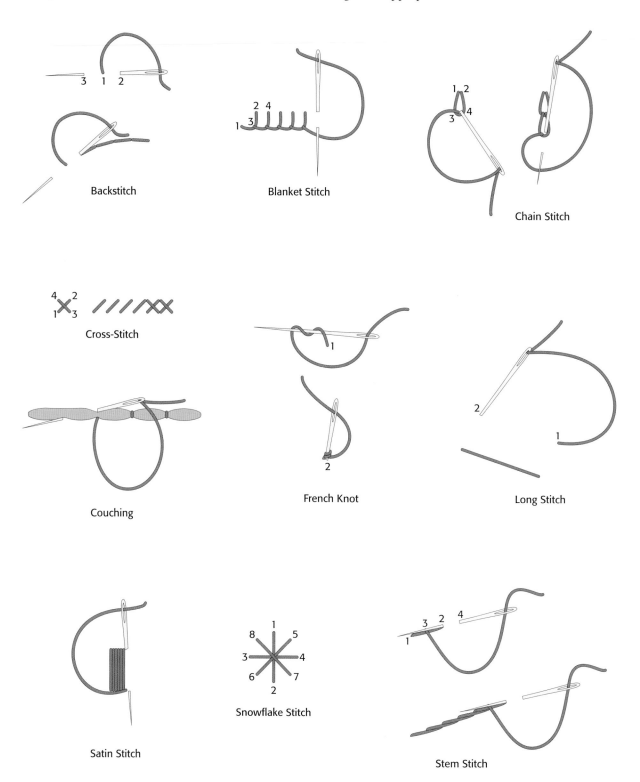

Backstitch

Blanket Stitch

Chain Stitch

Cross-Stitch

Couching

French Knot

Long Stitch

Satin Stitch

Snowflake Stitch

Stem Stitch

Embellishments

One of the fun aspects of making the fabric projects in this book is the opportunity to experiment with different techniques to embellish them. The whimsical designs will inspire you to use thread work, painting, stamping, beading, and quilting to create your own unique projects. The designs are whimsical, and adding vividly colored threads with embroidery, beads or bangles, and colorful painted or stamped details add to the originality of your project.

Free-Motion Machine Embroidery

I've been fascinated with free-motion embroidery for several years now. I consider it a new way for me to draw and paint with thread instead of a pencil or brush. It's also a way to create wonderful texture and movement on fabric. My first attempts at this technique were awkward and primitive, but I was hooked from the start. Though I use a straight-stitch setting most of the time, I am beginning to experiment with free-motion zigzag stitching now. What fun! I used to think that free-motion embroidery was a new technique. After doing much reading and research, I have learned that women have been using it for many years; we just have better tools and technology today.

For the uninitiated, free-motion embroidery is a machine-stitching technique that allows you to move the fabric freely under a darning foot of the sewing machine. Because the feed dogs are lowered or covered, the stitch length and direction of the stitching is controlled by you rather than by the machine. It is similar to the techniques of drawing with a pencil or painting with a fine-tip brush.

Darning Foot

Embroidery needles, metallic needles, and top-stitching needles work best for free-motion embroidery. They're made specifically for stitching decorative threads, such as rayons, metallics, and others, smoothly.

When stitching with decorative threads, I like to use them with thread made specifically for bobbins. They're thin so you can fit a lot of thread on a bobbin at one time, which means you won't run out of thread quickly. Bobbin threads also have no stretch, which makes them a great companion to your decorative top thread. They're typically available in black and white only, however, so if the back of the piece is an important part of the project, you may want to use the same color of thread in the bobbin as is used on the top. In that case, try using a lightweight cotton thread, such as a 60-weight embroidery thread, that matches your decorative top thread.

When I first started doing machine embroidery, I often used an embroidery hoop to hold the fabric taut. I usually stabilize the fabric first with either an iron-on fusible interfacing or layers of thin cotton batting and muslin. I've also used fusible batting or fleece as a stabilizer for machine embroidery or quilting. I find the plastic embroidery hoop with the metal spring works best. You can also find wooden hoops made specifically for machine embroidery. The best sizes of hoops for machine work are 6" and 8". Any larger, and your hoop will be limited in its range of motion with the machine.

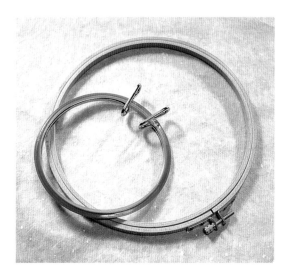

Choose a thin hoop that will easily fit under your machine needle.

Most times, I now work without a hoop. I've gained experience, and I usually work on smaller pieces so I have more control over moving the fabric. For the blocks in the book, some of the machine embroidery is done before the piece is layered and quilted. But, I also like to go back and add embroidery details after the basic outline, echo, or stipple quilting has been done.

I recommend that you work on a practice piece before doing free-motion embroidery or quilting on your project. Some time spent practicing will pay off well. Good ergonomics will help to ensure success: good lighting (Ott-Lites are great) and a comfortable, supportive chair are musts. I also recommend using quilting gloves to help cut down on the strain that can occur if you spend hours working in this technique. The little no-skid pads on the palms of the gloves mean that you don't have to put as much pressure on the fabric as you work. (See "Resources" on page 94 for these projects.)

Here are some tips to get the most from your practice session.

- Layer a piece of practice fabric with thin batting and a backing fabric similar to what you want to use in your project. The top layer may be a fun print that you can use to practice outlining with free-motion stitching. Or, choose a plain fabric and practice "writing" in cursive with the thread or make swirls, freeform flowers, and other shapes.

- Use a slower speed when using metallic or specialty threads to prevent breakage. Otherwise, I use a fairly fast needle speed with a slow and easy motion of the fabric. With experience, you will learn how to coordinate the speed and the motion of free-motion embroidery and quilting.

- Work oversized. Any time you do free-motion quilting or even hand quilting, it is best to start with fabric that is a bit larger than the size you want the finished piece to be. For example, the blocks in the book have a design area of 8" square. Heavy quilting and embellishing cause the fabric to pull in and "shrink" a bit, so I cut the original background square, batting, and backing fabrics to 10" square. The design elements on the top of the background fabrics also extended beyond the 8" square area. When the stitching and embellishing were complete, I trimmed the layers into an even 9" quilt block that included enough room to apply the ½" binding. The binding covers the raw edges of the overlapping appliqué shapes and frames the quilt block.

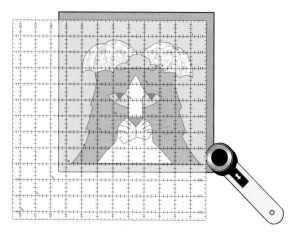

Trim oversized block to 9" square.

Quilt block with ¼" binding applied

Sampler of free-motion machine stitches.

Fabric Paints

The range of paints you can use on fabric today is amazing. I love to incorporate fabric painting in my work. Some of my favorites are Textile, Lumiere, and Neopaque paints from Jacquard Products. They can be applied using a brush, stamps, or stencils. I sometimes dilute the paints with water to create a wash or glaze to use on fabrics. There's no exact formula for diluting paints for use on fabric. Some paint companies make products that extend the paints without changing the color. I always recommend testing the paint after diluting it with water on a scrap of fabric. More diluted paint creates a thin wash of color. Add less water when a more opaque look is desired or to prepare a paint to be used for line work. I have used fabric paints extensively on several of the blocks in the book. Some other great paints are Jacquard's Dye-Na-Flow and Pébéo's Setacolor and Setacolor Soleil paints.

Use paints to add small areas of color where you may not want to appliqué or embroider something. For example, the facial features of the pumpkin hats on the October cat were painted. You can even use paint to cover up little mistakes! More details on fabric painting will be shared in the instructions for each quilt block.

If you don't have access to fabric paints, you can turn most acrylic paints into fabric paints by adding a textile medium, such as Delta's textile medium. A textile medium will make acrylic paints softer and more permanent on fabric surfaces. Always read the manu-facturer's directions for use and determine whether the paints need to be heat-set. See "Resources" for contact information on the various paint manufacturers.

Soft bristle brushes are best for fabric painting. The brush sizes you'll need depend on the size of your project. I recommend having a range of sizes of round and flat brushes as well as foam brushes for fabric painting.

Beads

Another fun way to embellish a quilted piece is to use beads. My favorites are seed beads and bugle beads. You'll need a durable thread for attaching beads, and I've tried everything from quilting thread to Nymo, which is a nylon thread made expressly for beading. I use the latter most often. You'll need a beading needle, too, which is long and thin and has an eye small enough to fit through the tiny holes in seed and bugle beads. Because the eyes are so small, you may also want a needle threader. Buttons are also popular embellishments, and the variety of buttons available today is amazing.

Stamps

Stamping is another great way to embellish fabric. You can even create a repeat on fabric with a stamp to make your own printed fabric. Stamping options include buying stamp pads for fabric stamping or applying Lumiere, Neopaque, or Textile paints with small sponges to the stamp. For larger shapes or to create your own textured stamps, it's easy to cut compressed sponges (available at crafts stores) with scissors into whatever shape you want. I used small heart stamps on the Heart Hats block on page 30.

Free-Motion Machine Quilting

The needle and thread recommendations for free-motion machine quilting are pretty much the same as for free-motion embroidery. However, you may want to use a slightly larger needle for stitching through all of the quilt layers, such as a size 90/14 instead of a 75/11 or 80/12. With free-motion quilting you can serve two purposes—quilting and embroidery. Using pretty threads while you quilt will let you add texture and design elements to your appliqué piece at the same time.

I use straight pins to baste the layers together and I move them out of the way as I am working. It is best to work from the center outward, checking the backing periodically to make sure it is not puckering. The quilting patterns I most often use are echo quilting, which follows the outline of the appliqué shapes, and stipple quilting, which is a small random pattern that's good for filling in blank areas in the design.

Echo Quilting

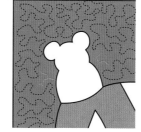

Stipple Quilting

Bindings, Battings, and Backings

As mentioned in "Free-Motion Machine Embroidery" on page 15, I always cut the block top, batting, and backing fabric slightly larger than I want my finished piece to be. For the blocks in the book, I cut them all 10" square, and the finished block size is 9" square. I prefer a low-loft cotton batting, such as Warm & Natural, because of its thickness and smoothness. A rotary cutter, cutting mat, and ruler are your best choice for precision cutting, but it is very important to be careful when using a rotary cutter. The blade should always be closed when not in use.

Binding a block or quilt finishes the edges and adds durability to the quilt and color to the design. There are different ways to do the binding, but an easy way for small projects is described here.

I prefer to use strips cut on the straight of the grain. If you don't have a long-enough piece of fabric to cut a continuous piece of binding, it can be pieced. For the small blocks in this book, you can cut one strip across the width of the fabric and it will be long enough to bind all four sides of a block, or you can cut binding on the lengthwise grain if you prefer.

To make ½"-wide finished binding, cut your binding strip 3" wide. If you don't have enough fabric left over to cut one long strip, cut several shorter ones, each 3" wide, and piece them together to make enough length to go all the way around your quilt top and have a little extra for mitering the corners and finishing the ends; a length of 42" or the width of the fabric will work just fine.

1. If necessary, piece the strips together end to end. Start by cutting the ends at a 45° angle to make it easy to align the ends and sew them together.

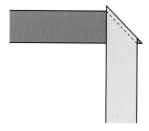

Cut binding strips at 45° angle
before sewing together.

2. Fold under one end of the binding strip ½" and press. Then fold the strip in half lengthwise, wrong sides together, and press.

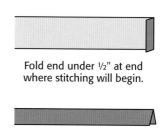

Fold end under ½" at end
where stitching will begin.

Fold binding strip in half lengthwise
before sewing onto quilt.

3. Starting a couple of inches from a corner, line up the raw edges of binding, beginning with the end that was folded under, with the raw edges of the block. Begin stitching a couple of inches from the folded-under edge of the binding, using a ½" seam allowance. Stop sewing ½" from the first corner, backstitch, and cut the threads. Fold the binding at a 45º angle, up and away from the block. Fold the binding strip back down so it is in line with the raw edges of the block and begin stitching the next side ½" from the edge. Repeat this process until all four corners are sewn.

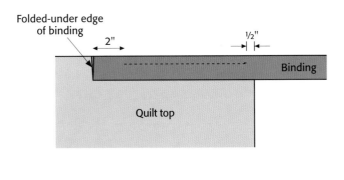

Folded-under edge of binding

2"

½"

Binding

Quilt top

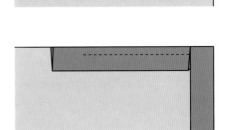

4. When approaching the initial folded end of the binding, determine where to cut off the tail end of the binding strip, allowing approximately ½" of binding to insert into the fold of the starting point. Once the tail is inserted so the raw edges are encased, continue stitching the binding in place.

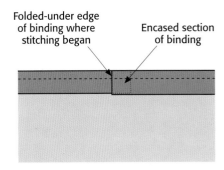

Folded-under edge of binding where stitching began

Encased section of binding

5. To complete the binding, fold it over to the back of the quilt, covering the line of machine stitches, and hand stitch it in place.

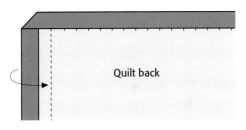

Quilt back

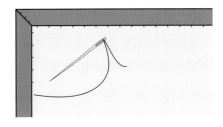

The cat designs are well suited for painting. They may be reduced or enlarged to suit your own needs. Always choose the proper paints and materials for your projects. Consult your local arts or crafts store staff for advice.

Painting on Glass

Some glass paints require low-temperature baking in an oven to heat-set the colors. Others are air-dry paints. Read the manufacturer's directions before using them. Most paints are for decorative use only, and the surfaces of the painted piece should not come in contact with food. The vase shown above and on

Painting Techniques

page 49 was painted with Pébéo's Vitrea paints, which are heat-set in the oven. The ornaments and light catchers featuring the January and December designs on page 91 were painted with Delta's PermEnamel glass paints. They air-dry and cure without baking.

Before painting, wash the glass item in warm, soapy water. Dry each piece with a clean towel and set it aside. If there is any dirt or oil on the surface, the paint won't adhere properly.

Transferring Patterns

To transfer the pattern onto your glassware, you can either put your pattern underneath or inside the glass item and use it as a guide for painting. Or, you can use a china marker to draw the design on the surface before painting. China markers look like pencils, but they are waxy and easily rub off of glass surfaces. For ceramics, you'll need graphite paper or transfer paper so that you can trace over the pattern and transfer the design onto the opaque surface. Make sure the pattern fits the glassware you're working with. If necessary, enlarge or reduce the pattern on a photocopier to fit your glass piece.

Supplies and Techniques

It's a good idea to practice first, before beginning your project. As long as the paints aren't heat-set, you can remove them with water or rubbing alcohol. So, you can practice on your actual piece or on a separate piece of glass. I use a variety of soft brushes—flats, rounds, and liner brushes—in various sizes. The project directions specify what type of brushes you will need.

If you plan to use outline paint, apply it first. Then you can fill in the area of color with a brush or sponge. The angle at which you hold the brush will affect how the paint flows onto the glass. The amount of pressure you use is also a factor. I often hold my brush almost flat against the surface as I work, exerting very little pressure, because I find I get better paint coverage. This technique is hard to do with a stiff brush, so be sure to use soft brushes.

Heat-Setting

Make sure you heat-set glass paints according to the manufacturer's instructions before using your finished project.

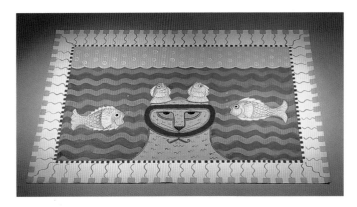

A whimsical canvas floorcloth makes a fun addition to a bathroom or child's bedroom.

Painting on Papier-Mâché, Wood, and Canvas

One of the projects in this book is painted on papier-mâché, one on wood, and one on canvas. There is also a painted plaque that is used as a decorative hanger for the blocks of the month. The February design is painted on a heart-shaped papier-mâché box, the November design adds color and fun to a wooden tray, and the August design was enlarged to create a floorcloth. For all three projects, the surfaces were prepared with a layer of gesso. Unless you are staining wood before painting a design, it is best to prime it with gesso or some type of wood primer.

Prepping Canvas

If you're making a floorcloth, the easiest approach is to purchase preprimed canvas. The gesso on the top and bottom surfaces stabilizes the canvas and prevents warping and shrinking. If you use raw canvas, choose one that is a heavier weight, such as #10 artist's canvas. Cut it a few inches larger than the finished floorcloth dimensions and prime each side with gesso before cutting the actual floorcloth. Also, after cutting out the primed canvas, add gesso to the edges of the canvas so all areas are primed. (I apply gesso to the edges of the preprimed canvas, too, to seal them.)

With each successive coat of paint or varnish, the edges are also coated. In addition, I paint a 2"- to 3"-wide border on the back of floorcloths and varnish the border to make it durable, rather than hemming the cloth. I prefer the nice flat edges, but of course, this is a matter of personal preference. A brush-on product, available at some craft stores, can be applied to the back of the floorcloth to prevent it from slipping, or you can simply cut a piece of nonskid mat for use under throw rugs and place it underneath your floorcloth.

Transferring Patterns

After enlarging or reducing the pattern to fit the size of the surface to be painted, you need to transfer the design to your surface. Use graphite paper or transfer paper. Or, make your own transfer paper by rubbing a soft pencil or chalk onto the back of the pattern. Then, position the paper on the papier-mâché, wood, or canvas and trace over the pattern lines with a pencil to transfer the design.

Supplies and Techniques

Many good-quality acrylic craft paints are available today. One of the best is the Delta Ceramcoat line. It offers a huge selection of colors and several accessory products to make painting easier. It's especially fun to experiment with such things as glazing liquids and metallic paints.

Try painting on papier-mâché for a one-of-a-kind gift.

Using good-quality brushes, such as those from Loew-Cornell, will also help to ensure success. It is important to clean the brushes well periodically as you are using them. Reshape the ends with soapy water and allow them to dry. This soapy film will help to maintain the shape of the brush and won't harm them in any way. Brushes should always be stored in an upright position after cleaning. I recommend keeping a variety of shapes and sizes of brushes on hand. Flat brushes and shader brushes (also flat) are recommended for painting larger areas of color and for filling in solid shapes. Flat brushes are usually labeled according to the width of the brush in inches. Round brushes are labeled in numbers: the higher the number, the larger the brush. They are also used for painting solid shapes as well as for things like stroke work and dots. Those labeled 0 and 00 are smaller and are made for detail work. Liner brushes are also round and are necessary for painting fine lines and details. Synthetic bristle brushes are most often used for craft painting. Consult your local arts and crafts store staff for more information on brushes.

When painting, think in terms of working from background to foreground. Paint the base color of each shape before starting any layering or detail work. The real fun begins after all of the base coats are completed. Creating interesting color, texture, and pattern will make yours a one-of-a-kind project.

Besides painting with brushes, try out different types of sponges, stamps, and stencils, too. Experiment by masking areas of the project with tape to create different patterns.

Glazes are simple and effective ways to add design and dimension to your painting. The details of how glazes were used for each project are given in the project instructions. There is no exact formula for mixing glazes that are transparent or semi-transparent layers of color. They can be made by mixing paints with water or with a combination of a glazing liquid and water. It is best to experiment by mixing glazes and testing them on a scrap of wood, canvas, or material similar to the project you are working on. Add additional paint for a more opaque look. Add glazing liquid and water for a more transparent look or if a wash of color is preferred. For line or detail work, add just enough water or glazing liquid to improve the flow of the paint.

Water-based varnishes are used to complete each project. They're easy to use and available in satin, gloss, and matte finishes. I used a satin interior varnish for all the painted finishes in this book. The type of finish is a matter of personal preference. Follow the manufacturer's instructions for varnishing. When working with wood, it's a good idea to sand lightly with fine sandpaper between coats of varnish. If you discover a mistake in the painting after varnishing, repaint and varnish over it again.

Painting on Nylon

I used regular acrylic paints on the umbrella (page 43) because they don't need to be heat-set. I would worry about damaging the nylon with an iron, so I didn't use fabric paints, which need to be heat-set.

All of the designs in the book have been made as quilt blocks that can hang from brass hooks on a painted wooden plaque. I sewed small plastic curtain rings to the two upper corners of the blocks to match the placement of the hooks on the plaque.

The plaque shown is painted, but other options for decorating a plaque include staining the wood, stenciling, or stamping. Color is a matter of personal preference. The example shown on page 24 and below is painted black with several accent colors. It works well with the many colors in my quilt blocks, as well as with the decor of my home. You may prefer to paint three or four plaques for the different seasons of the year. Another option is to sew a single curtain ring to the back of the blocks and hang them directly on the wall.

The materials listed for the quilt projects are for 9" blocks with 8" of design area and a ½" binding around each. If you prefer larger blocks, simply enlarge the designs. Of course, if you make bigger blocks, you'll need more fabric than is indicated in the materials list for each little quilt.

If you'd prefer, you can stitch all the blocks together to create a block-of-the-month quilt. Another option is to make a wall hanging that features the blocks representing the birthday months of family members or other special people in your life. Or enlarge a design or two and stitch them into throw pillows. The possibilities are endless.

Besides making the blocks from cotton fabrics, the designs will work well in silks, woolens, or felt. For example, the January block is shown made in cotton as well as in silk on page 28. The October block is shown as a felt purse on page 77. You may even want to reduce the designs and appliqué them on clothing or home-decorating projects. The shapes to be appliquéd are numbered in the order in which they are to be fused in place.

PROJECTS

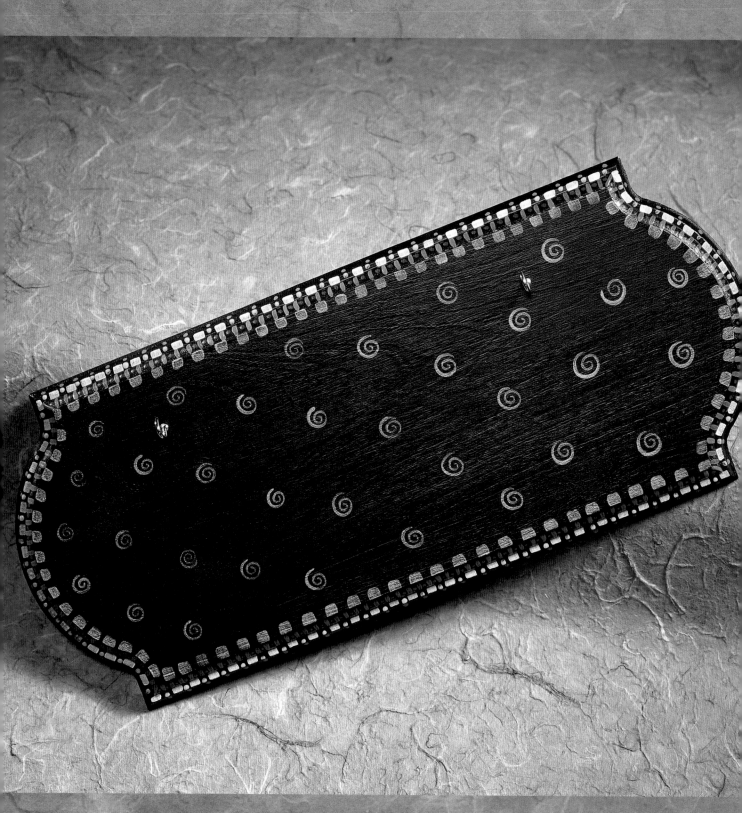

Hanging Plaque

The plaque is first painted black, and then additional colors are used to make dots-and-dashes designs around the shaped edges of the wood. Gold accents on the surface complete the design.

Materials

- Plaque: Innkeeper Sign #14071 by Walnut Hollow, 6" x 14" (see "Resources" on page 94)

- Fine sandpaper

- Gesso

- Delta Ceramcoat acrylic paints in Black, White, Napthol Crimson, Raspberry, Bright Yellow, Vibrant Green, Denim Blue, and Metallic 14K Gold

- Delta Ceramcoat satin indoor varnish

- Paintbrushes: 1" wash, #8 shader for checks, #0 liner brush for thin lines and small dots around edges of plaque

- 2 small brass cup hooks

- Hanging hardware for back of plaque

Painting the Plaque

1. Lightly sand the plaque and remove dust.
2. Apply one coat of gesso with the 1" brush to the front and back of the plaque. Lightly sand again with fine sandpaper.
3. Apply one coat of black paint to the entire front and back of the plaque, using the 1" brush.
4. With the shader brush, paint gold and white checks around the edges of the plaque, referring to the photograph.

5. With the liner brush, paint pink, red, blue, and yellow dots and lines on the edges.
6. With the liner brush, paint gold swirls on the top surface of the plaque.
7. With the 1" brush, apply two to three coats of the satin varnish.
8. Measure the plaque to mark the placement of the brass hooks. Mine are placed about 7" apart and 1" down from the top edge of the plaque. Screw the hooks into position.
9. Apply hanging hardware to the back of the plaque.

JANUARY

Cold as Mice Quilt Block

This fellow is quite content to have snow mice on his ears. The easy appliqué shapes are enhanced with echo quilting in the cat body and the blue sky background. I used stipple quilting to give texture to the snow, and the trees get their texture from free-motion straight stitches. The tree trunks and snow-mice arms were made using a satin stitch. I hand stitched the snowflakes using white pearl cotton and added some shimmer to the block by painting sparkle white paint onto the mice and by dabbing the same paint here and there on the snowflakes and the white background. As a final touch, I sewed on black seed beads for the mice features.

Materials

Yardage is based on 42"-wide fabric.

- 10" square of blue fabric for block background
- 6" x 10" scrap of tan fabric for cat
- Scraps of white, cream, dark green, dark brown, black, and yellow fabrics for appliqué details
- ⅛ yard of green fabric for binding
- 10" square of backing fabric
- 10" square of low-loft cotton batting
- ½ yard of Steam-A-Seam 2 fusible web
- ⅜ yard of stabilizer
- Tracing paper or acetate
- Black permanent pen
- Jacquard Lumiere Paint in Super Sparkle White
- Paintbrushes: #8 shader, #0 liner
- Threads for machine embroidery in desired colors
- Bobbin thread
- Skein of white pearl cotton or embroidery floss
- 16 black seed beads, beading thread, and beading needle for mice faces
- 2 small plastic curtain rings

Preparation

Read the "Fusible Appliqué" section on page 10 before beginning.

1. Enlarge the Cold as Mice pattern (page 29) 110% on a photocopier.
2. Prepare an overlay or positioning guide by tracing the entire enlarged design onto acetate or tracing paper with a permanent pen.
3. Turn the overlay to the wrong side and trace each individual appliqué pattern piece (they'll be in reverse) onto either side of the Steam-A-Seam 2 fusible web. The shapes are numbered in the order that they should be appliquéd. Cut around the shapes on the fusible web, leaving a ⅛" to ¼" allowance around the drawn line.
4. Starting with piece 1, remove the paper layer from the opposite side of the drawn shape and discard. Hand press the fusible web with the pattern onto the back of the fabric you want to use for that appliqué shape. Do not iron in place yet.
5. Cut out the fabric, following the drawn lines on the paper layer and leaving the paper layer intact. Set aside. Repeat steps 4 and 5 for each shape to be appliquéd.
6. Place the acetate or tissue-paper overlay on the 10" blue background fabric square, referring to "Fusible Appliqué." The blue fabric will be the base for the other fabrics.

7. Working in numerical order, remove the paper layer from each shape and position it in place before ironing down permanently. Overlap where necessary.

8. With an iron, press all shapes into position, following the manufacturer's instructions for the fusible web.

Appliqué and Embellishment

1. Iron or pin stabilizer to the back of the block.

2. Use a machine satin stitch or blanket stitch, or hand stitch around each shape in the desired thread colors. Working from the background to the foreground, continue until all shapes have been appliquéd, except for the trees.

3. Use a satin stitch to create the twig arms of the mice, the tree trunks, and the facial details in the cat. I used brown thread for these details.

4. Remove the stabilizer from the back of the block. A hemostat or tweezers will make this task much easier.

5. Layer the quilt block with the 10" squares of batting and backing fabric. Pin all three layers together with the block right side up on top, the batting in the middle, and the backing fabric on the bottom, right side down.

6. Quilt the layers by machine or by hand. I used blue thread to echo quilt around the top of the cat and the mice in the sky background, and tan thread to echo quilt in the cat's body. I stipple quilted the snow.

7. Using green thread that is slightly lighter than the appliquéd trees, free-motion stitch to create shape and texture in the trees.

8. Hand embroider the snowflakes, following the snowflake stitch diagram on page 14.

9. Sew black seed beads to create the faces of the snow mice, using beading thread and a beading needle.

10. Paint the snow mice with the sparkling white paint with the shader brush. Dab the paint onto the trees, embroidered snowflakes, and snow background with the liner brush. Heat-set the paint according to the manufacturer's directions.

Finishing

1. Use a ruler and rotary cutter to trim the block to 9" x 9".

2. Cut a 3" x 42" strip of green fabric for binding and attach it, following the directions on page 18.

3. Sew the curtain rings to the back of the block, aligning them to correspond with the cup hooks on the plaque.

Silk and Glass Options

The Cold as Mice design is shown top right stitched in silk fabrics and embellished with paint, beads, and free-motion embroidery and quilting. The silks give the project an added shimmer. The design would also work well in felt and could be used to embellish a wool scarf or mittens. Simply reduce or enlarge the pattern to the desired size and appliqué the felt pieces by hand, using a blanket stitch and an outline stitch.

Another fun way to use this design is as a glass ornament or sun catcher (bottom right) to brighten up the winter season. I reduced the pattern and painted it on a purchased glass circle. For complete instructions on making the glass ornament, see page 91.

Cold as Mice
Enlarge pattern 110% for quilt block.
Reduce pattern 59% for glass ornament.

FEBRUARY

Heart Hats Quilt Block

The heart hats these cats are wearing express their "mewtual" affection. The techniques used for this block include appliqué, stamping with metallic paints, free-motion embroidery, and quilting. Echo quilting outlines the cat faces as well as the background areas.

Directions for a companion project, a painted papier-mâché box, follow the quilt-block instructions. It is just one of many possibilities for this design. Another idea you might try is to reduce the size of the design and cut the shapes from different papers to make a special card for your valentine. Stamping can add color and interest to a paper design. And why not frame the card and display it in a special place to be enjoyed for a long time? This design would also work well for a wedding or anniversary gift. You could even include names and a date in the design.

Materials

Yardage is based on 42"-wide fabric.

- 10" square of dark red fabric for background
- Scraps of black, gray, yellow, green, and pink fabrics for appliqué details
- 1/8 yard of pink fabric for binding
- 10" square of backing fabric
- 10" square of low-loft batting
- 1/2 yard of Steam-A-Seam 2 fusible web
- 3/8 yard of stabilizer
- Tracing paper or acetate
- Black permanent pen
- Jacquard Lumiere paint in Pearlescent Magenta
- Small- and medium-size heart rubber stamps or small, round paintbrush
- Makeup sponge
- Threads for machine embroidery in desired colors
- Bobbin thread
- 2 small plastic curtain rings

Preparation

Read the "Fusible Appliqué" section on page 10 before beginning.

1. Enlarge the Heart Hats pattern (page 35) 110% on a photocopier.
2. Prepare an overlay or positioning guide by tracing the entire enlarged design onto acetate or tracing paper with a permanent pen.
3. Turn the overlay to the wrong side and trace each individual appliqué pattern piece (they'll be in reverse) onto one side of the paper layer of the Steam-A-Seam 2 fusible web. The shapes are numbered in the order that they should be appliquéd. Cut around the shapes on the fusible web, leaving a 1/8" to 1/4" allowance around the drawn line.
4. Starting with piece 1, remove the paper layer from the opposite side of the drawn shape and discard. Hand press the fusible with the pattern onto the back of the fabric you want to use for that appliqué shape. Do not iron in place yet.
5. Cut out the fabric, following the drawn lines on the paper and leaving the paper intact. Set aside. Repeat steps 4 and 5 for each shape to be appliquéd.

6. Place the acetate or tissue-paper overlay on the 10" dark red background square, referring to "Fusible Appliqué" on page 10. The red fabric will be the base for the other fabrics.

7. Working in numerical order, remove the paper layer from each shape and position it in place before ironing down permanently. Overlap where necessary.

8. With an iron, press all shapes into position, following the manufacturer's instructions for the fusible web.

Appliqué and Embellishment

1. Iron or pin stabilizer to the back of the block.

2. Use a machine satin stitch or blanket stitch, or hand stitch around each shape in the desired thread colors. Working from the background to the foreground, continue until all shapes have been appliquéd.

3. Using a makeup sponge, apply the magenta paint to a small heart stamp and practice stamping onto a scrap of fabric before stamping onto the hats and block background between the cats. If desired, you may paint the hearts by hand with a small round brush. Reapply paint after stamping each heart.

4. Again using the sponge, apply the same paint to the larger heart stamp. Stamp the tip of each hat, overlapping the shapes in the middle of the block. The larger hearts may also be painted by hand following the shapes on the printed pattern.

5. Remove the stabilizer from the back of the block. A hemostat or tweezers will make this task much easier.

6. Layer the quilt block with the 10" squares of batting and backing fabric. Pin all three layers together with the block right side up on top, the batting in the middle, and the backing fabric on the bottom, right side down.

7. Quilt the layers together by machine or by hand. I used gray thread to echo quilt the cats' faces, and pink metallic thread to echo quilt the background areas.

Finishing

1. Use a ruler and rotary cutter to trim the block to 9" x 9".

2. Cut a 3" x 42" strip of pink fabric for binding and attach it, following the directions on page 18.

3. Sew the curtain rings to the back of the block, aligning them to correspond with the cup hooks on the plaque.

Heart Hats Painted Papier-Mâché Box

These friendly felines work well on the heart-shaped box, but the design would look nice on a round or square box, too. The pattern was reduced before being traced onto the prepared surface. There's plenty of room in the box for chocolates or other tokens of affection.

Materials

- 9" x 9" x 4½" purchased heart-shaped papier-mâché box (available at Jo-Ann Stores; see "Resources" on page 94)

- Gesso

- Delta Ceramcoat acrylic paints in Black, White, Opaque Red, Wild Rose, Crocus Yellow, and Wedgwood Green

- Delta Ceramcoat Clear Glaze Base

- Delta Ceramcoat satin interior varnish

- Jacquard Lumiere paint in Halo Pink Gold

- Pencil

- Tracing paper or graphite paper (optional)

- Paintbrushes: 1" wash brush, #4 flat, #1 round, #18/0 liner, ¾" flat, #0 round

- Heart stamps (optional)

Preparation

1. Apply one coat of gesso to the exteriors of the box and the box lid using the 1" brush. Allow to dry thoroughly.
2. Reduce the pattern, opposite, to fit your box. For a 9" heart-shaped box, it will need to be reduced to 88%. If you're using a larger or smaller box, you'll need to change the proportions accordingly.
3. Referring to the information on page 22, transfer the design to the box lid.

Painting the Box

1. Using the 1" brush and red paint, paint the large exterior areas of the top and bottom of the box. Use the #4 flat brush for the smaller red areas.
2. Paint one cat's eyes yellow and the other cat's eyes green, using the #1 brush.
3. Paint the left cat black, and then mix black and white paint together and use it to paint the right cat gray with the #4 flat brush. Using the same brush, paint the lighter area of the black cat gray.
4. Mix a white glaze using equal parts of the glaze base and white paint. Test before applying. Add more paint if you want more white to show. Add more glaze if you want a more transparent glaze. Paint texture and details on cats, using the white glaze and the #0 round brush.
5. Dilute the black paint with a small amount of water to make it flow more easily and use it and the #18/0 liner brush to paint face details and the black pupils of the cats' eyes. Add white highlights in the cats' eyes with the same brush.
6. Paint the hats, using the #1 brush and rose paint.
7. Dilute the Halo Pink Gold paint with water to create a wash (use approximately equal parts paint and water) and apply to the hats with the #0 round brush. Paint the heart shapes between the cats and on top of the hats with the full strength Halo Pink Gold paint using the #0 brush.
8. Paint small hearts on the hats with red paint and the liner brush or use heart-shaped stamps.
9. Prepare a glaze with equal parts of the rose paint and glaze base. Paint lines around the cats with the pink glaze and the #0 round brush.
10. Use the same pink glaze and the #4 flat brush to paint stripes freehand around the sides of the box top. Use the same glaze and the ¾" flat brush to paint wider stripes on the sides of the box bottom.
11. Apply two or three coats of the interior varnish to the entire inside and outside of the box and lid.

Paint

6

3

5

4

1

2

9

11

15

17

16

14

10

12

7

13

(7)

18

8

Embroidery

Heart Hats
Enlarge pattern 110% for quilt block.
Reduce pattern 88% for papier-mâché box.

Note: Piece 7 is one piece with cat's eyes and nose appliquéd on top of it.

MARCH **Windy Kitty Quilt Block**

This cool cat is an ambitious kite flyer who has taken advantage of a windy situation. Notice how even his whiskers are blowing in the wind! First, I fused the cat, cloud, and fish shapes in place and satin stitched them. Next, I added details to the fish kites, stitching gold scales and facial details on top of the yellow fabric. I then satin stitched tree trunks by machine—simply increasing the width of the stitching near the base of the trunk to make them look more realistic.

Once the block was layered with batting and backing fabric, I added more thread details. The green triangle shapes of the trees were fused in place and embellished with free-motion quilting in light and dark green threads to make it appear that they are also blowing in the breeze. Finally, I added swirls when quilting the cloud and the sky to accentuate the feeling of movement. A fun, crayon-box colored plaid binding adds the final touch of springtime whimsy to Windy Kitty.

Materials

Yardage is based on 42"-wide fabric.

- 10" square of light blue fabric for background
- 4" x 10" scrap of green fabric for grass
- 6" x 10" scrap of brown polka-dot fabric for cat
- Scraps of black, yellow, white, and dark green fabrics for appliqué details
- ⅛ yard of plaid fabric for binding
- 10" square of backing fabric
- 10" square of low-loft cotton batting
- ½ yard of Steam-A-Seam 2 fusible web
- ⅜ yard of stabilizer
- Tracing paper or acetate
- Black permanent pen
- Threads for machine embroidery in desired colors
- Bobbin thread
- 2 small plastic curtain rings

Preparation

Read the "Fusible Appliqué" section on page 10 before beginning.

1. Enlarge the Windy Kitty pattern (page 39) 110% on a photocopier.
2. Prepare an overlay or positioning guide by tracing the entire enlarged design onto acetate or tracing paper with a permanent pen.
3. Turn the overlay to the wrong side and trace each individual appliqué pattern piece (they'll be in reverse) onto one side of the paper layer of the Steam-A-Seam 2 fusible web. The shapes are numbered in the order that they should be appliquéd. Cut around the shapes on the fusible web, leaving a ⅛" to ¼" allowance around the drawn line.
4. Starting with piece 1, remove the paper layer from the opposite side of the drawn shape and discard. Hand press the fusible with the pattern onto the back of the fabric you want to use for that appliqué shape. Do not iron in place yet.
5. Cut out the fabric, following the drawn lines on the paper layer and leaving the paper layer intact. Set aside. Repeat steps 4 and 5 for each shape to be appliquéd.

6. Place the acetate or tissue-paper overlay on the 10" light blue background square, referring to "Fusible Appliqué" on page 10. The blue fabric will be the base for the other fabrics.

7. Working in numerical order, remove the paper layer from each shape and position it in place before ironing down permanently. Overlap where necessary.

8. With an iron, press all shapes into position, following the manufacturer's instructions for the fusible web.

Note: The trees were made by fusing dark green shapes in place and then doing free motion stitching over the shapes in light and dark green threads.

Appliqué and Embellishment

1. Iron or pin stabilizer to the back of the block.

2. Use a machine satin stitch or blanket stitch, or hand stitch around each shape in the desired thread colors. Working from the background to the foreground, continue until all shapes have been appliquéd, except for the trees, which are created with satin stitching on the trunks and free-motion stitching over the dark green shapes.

3. Use a narrow satin stitch to create the kite strings and kite tails (I used blue thread), to stitch the ear details and whiskers on the cat (tan thread), and to stitch the tree trunks (brown thread). I used gold thread to add scales and facial details to the fish kites and a bit of red thread in satin stitch to add ties to the kite tails.

4. Remove the stabilizer from the back of the block. A hemostat or tweezers will make this task much easier.

5. Layer the quilt block with the 10" squares of batting and backing fabric. Pin all three layers together with the block right side up on top, the batting in the middle, and the backing fabric on the bottom, right side down.

6. Quilt the layers together by machine or by hand. I used blue thread to quilt swirls in the sky, and white thread to quilt swirls on the cloud. Notice how the swirls go in the same direction as the kites and whiskers. The grass and cat were both quilted in an up-and-down pattern to make zigzag-style lines that create texture.

7. Above each tree trunk, I used first a lighter green and then a darker green thread and free-motion stitching over the dark green fabric triangles to help define the outline of an evergreen tree and to show the effects of the wind blowing to the right.

Finishing

1. Use a ruler and rotary cutter to trim the block to 9" x 9".

2. Cut a 3" x 42" strip of plaid fabric for binding and attach it, following the directions on page 18.

3. Sew the curtain rings to the back of the block, aligning them to correspond with the cup hooks on the plaque.

Windy Kitty
Enlarge pattern 110%.

APRIL

Don't Rain on My Purrade
Quilt Block

The rain doesn't seem to be dampening this fellow's spirits. Perhaps it's because it's a spring rain full of promise for great days of fishing ahead. His umbrellas are accented with seed beads and bugle beads. The quilting in the background was stitched in undulating rows using Sulky's Holoshimmer thread to simulate rain. I used the same thread in a different color to hand stitch the shiny rain drops.

As a fun companion for this project, why not make the painted umbrella from the same designs? Complete directions for the umbrella start on page 43.

Materials

Yardage is based on 42"-wide fabric.

- 10" square of blue fabric for background
- 8" x 10" scrap of orange fabric for cat
- Scraps of beige, brown, green, and black fabrics for appliqué details
- ¼ yard of floral print for umbrellas and binding
- 10" square of backing fabric
- 10" square of low-loft cotton batting
- ½ yard of Steam-A-Seam 2 fusible web
- ⅜ yard of stabilizer
- Tracing paper or acetate
- Black permanent pen
- Threads for machine embroidery in desired colors (Holoshimmer in blue and silver for rain)
- Bobbin thread
- 10 blue seed beads and 2 blue bugle beads, beading needle, and beading thread for umbrellas
- 2 small plastic curtain rings

Preparation

Read the "Fusible Appliqué" section on page 10 before beginning.

1. Enlarge the Don't Rain on My Purrade pattern (page 45) 110% on a photocopier.
2. Prepare an overlay or positioning guide by tracing the entire enlarged design onto acetate or tracing paper with a permanent pen.
3. Turn the overlay to the wrong side and trace each individual appliqué pattern piece (they'll be in reverse) onto one side of the paper layer of the Steam-A-Seam 2 fusible web. The shapes are numbered in the order that they should be appliquéd. Cut around the shapes on the fusible web, leaving a ⅛" to ¼" allowance around the drawn line.
4. Starting with piece 1, remove the paper layer from the opposite side of the drawn shape and discard. Hand press the fusible web with the pattern onto the back of the fabric you want to use for that appliqué shape. Do not iron in place yet.
5. Cut out the fabric, following the drawn lines on the paper layer and leaving the paper layer intact. Set aside. Repeat steps 4 and 5 for each shape to be appliquéd.

thread colors. Working from the background to the foreground, continue until all shapes have been appliquéd.

3. Use a narrow satin stitch to appliqué the cat shapes and add the mouth and whisker details. I used brown thread.

4. Remove the stabilizer from the back of the block. A hemostat or tweezers will make this task much easier.

5. Layer the quilt block with the 10" squares of batting and backing fabric. Pin all three layers together with the block right side up on top, the batting in the middle, and the backing fabric on the bottom, right side down.

6. Quilt the layers together by machine or by hand. I stitched the background with wavy or undulating lines. To do this, I first drew straight vertical lines on the fabric at ¾" intervals with a white chalk pencil. I used these lines as guides while stitching with the Holoshimmer thread. Then I quilted the cat with up-and-down lines of straight stitches to create a zigzag effect that simulates fur. To give the umbrellas lots of definition, I quilted them inside and outside along the blue satin stitches. Finally, I echo quilted the cat's eyes.

7. To create raindrops, hand stitch single chain stitches (see page 14) using silver Holoshimmer thread.

8. Sew blue seed beads to the lower points of the umbrella, and a blue bugle bead to the top of each umbrella.

Finishing

1. Use a ruler and rotary cutter to trim the block to 9" x 9".

2. Cut a 3" x 42" strip of floral print for binding and attach it, following the directions on page 18.

3. Sew the curtain rings to the back of the block, aligning them to correspond with the cup hooks on the plaque.

6. Place the acetate or tissue-paper overlay on the 10" blue background square, referring to "Fusible Appliqué" on page 10. The blue fabric will be the base for the other fabrics.

7. Working in numerical order, remove the paper layer from each shape and position it in place before ironing down permanently. Overlap where necessary.

8. With an iron, press all shapes into position, following the manufacturer's instructions for the fusible web.

Appliqué and Embellishment

1. Iron or pin stabilizer to the back of the block.

2. Use a machine satin stitch or blanket stitch, or hand stitch around each shape in the desired

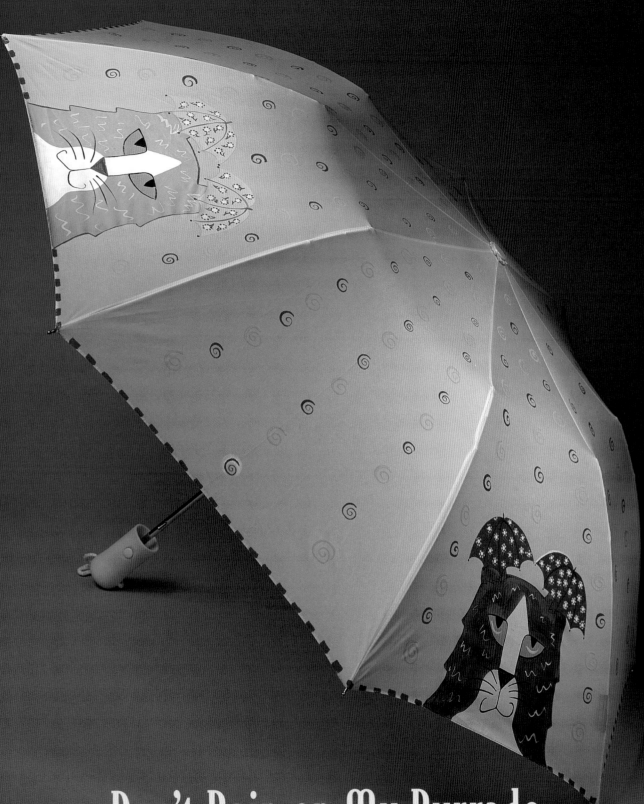

Don't Rain on My Purrade
Painted Umbrella

These purrading kitties can be painted on an umbrella to decorate for a wedding or baby shower. Because the nylon is treated, the project is for decorative use only. Another option is to paint the design on a cotton or silk umbrella, adding a fabric medium to the acrylic paints. However, these types of umbrellas are for protection on a sunny day as they are not waterproof.

Materials

- Light-colored umbrella
- Pencil
- Delta Ceramcoat acrylic paints in Dark Goldenrod, Light Ivory, Spice Brown, Dunes Beige, Wedgwood Green, Opaque Red, Crocus Yellow, Blue Heaven, Seminole Green, Black, Wedgwood Blue, and Tomato Spice
- Paintbrushes: #4 flat, #1 round

Preparation

1. Enlarge the Don't Rain on My Purrade pattern, opposite, 110% on a photocopier.
2. Place the pattern in position under the umbrella, centering it along the edge of one section. Support the pattern with a book or tray beneath it.
3. Trace the design lightly in pencil onto the outer surface of the umbrella. Repeat, tracing the design on every other section for a total of four cats.

Painting the Umbrella

1. With the flat brush, paint the eyes of two of the cats Seminole Green and the eyes of the other two cats goldenrod.
2. Using the flat brush, paint the two green-eyed cats goldenrod and the two orange-eyed cats brown.
3. Using the flat brush, paint the light area of the orange cats ivory and the light area of the brown cats beige.
4. With the #1 brush, paint the noses of all four cats brown.

5. Using the flat brush, paint the brown cats' umbrellas with Opaque Red and the orange cats' umbrellas with Blue Heaven.
6. With the #1 brush, paint small flowers on the red umbrellas. Use yellow for the petals and blue for the flower centers.
7. Using the #1 brush, paint small flowers on the blue umbrellas. Use green for the stems and leaves, red for the petals, and yellow for the flower centers.
8. Using the #1 brush, paint the pupils of the cats' eyes black.
9. Dilute the black paint slightly with water and use it with the #1 brush to outline the cats' eyes, noses, mouths, and whiskers. Also use it to outline the brown cats' ears. Add black dots at the lower points of the red umbrellas.
10. Using the #1 brush, add lines on the blue umbrellas with diluted Wedgwood Blue paint and on the red umbrellas with Tomato Spice paint. Add red dots on the lower points of the blue umbrellas and a blue line at the top of the blue umbrellas with the #1 brush.
11. Paint yellow lines at the tops of the red umbrellas and in the eyes of the brown cats with the #1 brush.
12. Paint alternating swirls of slightly diluted Opaque Red and Blue Heaven over the entire umbrella, using the #1 brush.
13. With the flat brush, paint small checks using Opaque Red around the lower edge of the umbrella.
14. Paint texture lines on the cats, using the #1 brush and beige for the brown cats and light ivory for the orange cats.
15. Allow paint to dry thoroughly before using the umbrella.

Swirl
Pattern is full-size.

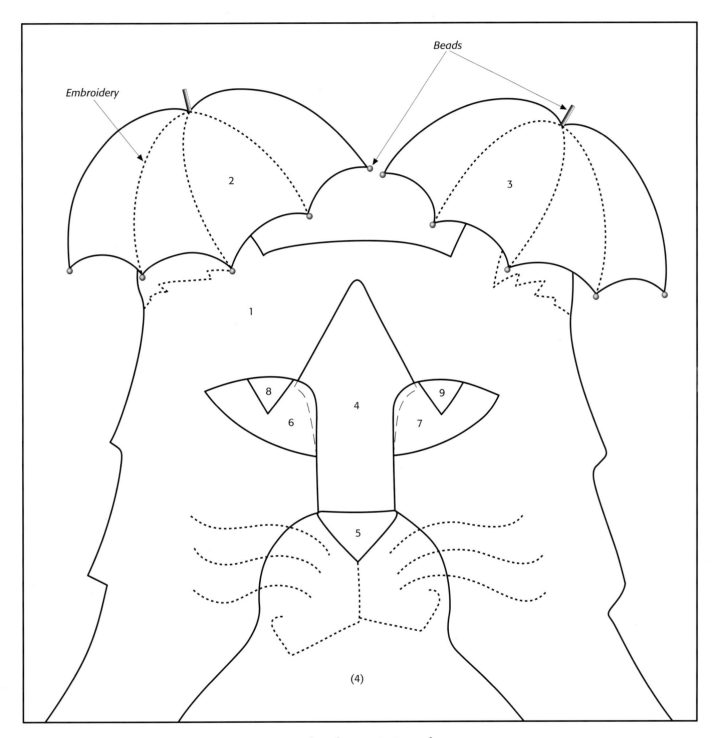

Don't Rain on My Purrade
Enlarge pattern 110%.

Note: Piece 4 is one piece with the nose (piece 5) appliquéd on top of it.

MAY Flowering Feline Quilt Block

This tabby has green eyes and appears to have a green thumb as well. I used simple stipple quilting in both the sky and grass background. The curving lines of the stitches seemed appropriate for both the rolling hills and a sky of patchy clouds. The cat features echo quilting, and for a finishing touch, the trees are embellished with seed beads.

Spring is such a wonderful season of hope and renewal. I couldn't resist making additional projects starring this character. Directions for a painted glass vase and a table runner begin on page 49.

Materials

Yardage is based on 42"-wide fabric.

- 10" square of blue fabric for background
- 6" x 10" scrap of light brown fabric for cat
- Scraps of medium green fabric for background, stems, and leaves
- Scraps of light green, dark green, cream, yellow, brown, and red fabrics for appliqué details
- ¼ yard of red gingham for binding and flowerpots
- 10" square of backing fabric
- 10" square of low-loft cotton batting
- ½ yard of Steam-A-Seam 2 fusible web
- ⅜ yard of stabilizer
- Tracing paper or acetate
- Black permanent pen
- Threads for machine embroidery in desired colors
- Bobbin thread
- 7 red and 5 yellow seed beads, beading thread, and beading needle for trees
- 2 small plastic curtain rings

Preparation

Read the "Fusible Appliqué" section on page 10 before beginning.

1. Enlarge the Flowering Feline pattern (page 54) 110% on a photocopier.
2. Prepare an overlay or positioning guide by tracing the entire enlarged design onto acetate or tracing paper with a permanent pen.
3. Turn the overlay to the wrong side and trace each individual appliqué pattern piece (they'll be in reverse) onto one side of the paper layer of the Steam-A-Seam 2 fusible web. The shapes are numbered in the order that they should be appliquéd. Cut around the shapes on the fusible web, leaving a ⅛" to ¼" allowance around the drawn line.
4. Starting with piece 1, remove the paper layer from the opposite side of the drawn shape and discard. Hand press the fusible web with the pattern onto the back of the fabric you want to use for that appliqué shape. Do not iron in place yet.
5. Cut out the fabric, following the drawn lines on the paper layer and leaving the paper layer intact. Set aside. Repeat steps 4 and 5 for each shape to be appliquéd.
6. Place the acetate or tissue-paper overlay on the 10" blue background square, referring to "Fusible Appliqué." The blue fabric will be the base for the other fabrics.

7. Working in numerical order, remove the paper layer from each shape and position it in place before ironing down permanently. Overlap where necessary.

8. With an iron, press all shapes into position, following the manufacturer's instructions for the fusible web.

Appliqué and Embellishment

1. Iron or pin stabilizer to the back of the block.

2. Use a machine satin stitch or blanket stitch, or hand stitch around each shape in the desired thread colors. Working from the background to the foreground, continue until all shapes have been appliquéd.

3. Use a narrow satin stitch to outline the cat's eyes, nose, mouth, and chin. I used brown thread. Outline the tan strips around his face and add whiskers. I used light tan thread.

4. Remove the stabilizer from the back of the block. A hemostat or tweezers will make this task much easier.

5. Layer the quilt block with the 10" squares of batting and backing fabric. Pin all three layers together with the block right side up on top, the batting in the middle, and the backing fabric on the bottom, right side down.

6. Quilt the layers together by machine or by hand. I used stipple quilting in both the blue and green backgrounds, and echo quilting in the cat. For the leaves, I used free-motion straight-line quilting to make veins. In the flowers, I quilted swirls in the center and then stitched zigzag circles around the centers.

7. Using the beading needle and beading thread, hand sew the red seed beads to the apple tree on the left and yellow seed beads to the pine tree on the right.

Finishing

1. Use a ruler and rotary cutter to trim the block to 9" x 9".

2. Cut a 3" x 42" strip of red gingham fabric for binding and attach it, following the directions on page 18.

3. Sew the curtain rings to the back of the block, aligning them to correspond with the cup hooks on the plaque.

Flowering Feline Painted Glass Vase

This vase will add a touch of spring to your decor any month of the year. It was painted with Pébéo's Vitrea glass paints and markers, which need to be heat-set in the oven.

Materials

- 9½" x 7⅜" Euro Vase #38858 52100 (available at Jo-Ann Stores; see "Resources" on page 94)

- Pébéo Vitrea 160 outliner in Ink Black and metal tip for applicator

- Pébéo Vitrea 160 glass paints in Veil White, Sun Yellow, Amber, Pepper Red, Mint Green, Azure Blue, and Ink Black

- Pébéo Vitrea 160 marker in Frosted Blue for swirls

- Paintbrushes: #0 liner, #3 round

- Tracing paper

- Tape

Preparation

1. Wash and dry the vase.
2. Enlarge the Flowering Feline pattern (page 54) to 110% and trace it onto tracing paper.
3. Position the pattern inside the vase and tape it in place. Stuff crumpled paper inside the vase to help hold the pattern flat against the inside of the surface to be painted.

Painting the Vase

1. Place the metal tip on the black outline paint tube and use it to outline the design. Allow the paint to dry.
2. Paint each outlined section in the desired colors. If you're right-handed, work from left to right to help avoid smearing paint with your hand. If you're left-handed, work in the opposite direction.
3. Draw swirls in the background of the vase on both sides using the frosted blue marker.
4. Allow the paint to dry for 24 hours before heat-setting. Follow the manufacturer's directions for heat-setting in the oven.

Flowering Feline Table Runner

This fun project features the Flowering Feline design at each end of the table runner. Set the table with this piece, put a bouquet of flowers in the painted vase, and you'll have a table like no one else. The fabrics in the table runner are from the Bloomin' Birds collection I designed for Clothworks fabrics. The colors are influenced by the clear blues, reds, yellows, and greens of Provence. Finished size is 14¾" x 42".

Materials

Yardage is based on 42"-wide fabric.

- 1⅜ yards of blue print for background
- ⅜ yard of yellow fabric for cats
- ⅜ yard of red floral for hills
- ⅜ yard of yellow print for border
- Scraps of red paisley for flowerpots
- Scraps of greens for eyes, stems, and leaves
- Scraps of yellow, red, and brown prints for appliqué details
- ⅜ yard of dark blue print for binding
- 1⅜ yards of backing fabric
- 18" x 45" piece of low-loft cotton batting
- 1½ yards of Steam-A-Seam 2 fusible web
- 1½ yards of stabilizer
- Acetate or tracing paper
- Black permanent pen
- Thread for machine embroidery in desired colors
- Bobbin thread

Preparation

Read the "Fusible Appliqué" section on page 10 before beginning.

1. Enlarge the Flowering Feline pattern (page 54) 137% on a photocopier.

2. Prepare an overlay or positioning guide by tracing the entire enlarged design onto acetate or tracing paper with a permanent pen.

3. Turn the overlay to the wrong side and trace each individual appliqué pattern piece (they'll be in reverse) onto one side of the paper layer of the Steam-A-Seam 2 fusible web. The shapes are numbered in the order that they should be appliquéd. Cut around the shapes on the fusible web, leaving a ⅛" to ¼" allowance around the drawn line. Repeat to make another set of shapes so you'll have one set for each end of the table runner.

4. Starting with piece 1, remove the paper layer from the opposite side of the drawn shape and discard. Hand press the fusible with the pattern onto the back of the fabric you want to use for that appliqué shape. Do not iron in place yet.

5. Cut out the fabric, following the drawn lines on the paper layer and leaving the paper layer intact. Set aside. Repeat steps 4 and 5 for each shape to be appliquéd.

6. Using a rotary cutter, mat, and ruler, cut a 12" x 40" piece from the blue print background fabric.

7. Place the acetate or tissue-paper overlay on one end of the background fabric, referring to "Fusible Appliqué."

8. Working in numerical order, remove the paper layer from each shape and position it in place before ironing down permanently. Overlap where necessary.

9. With an iron, press all shapes into position following the manufacturer's instructions for the fusible web.

10. Repeat steps 7–9 at the other end of the table runner.

Appliqué

1. Iron or pin stabilizer to the back of the areas to be appliquéd.

2. Use a machine satin stitch or blanket stitch, or hand stitch around each shape in the desired thread colors. Working from the background to the foreground, continue until all shapes have been appliquéd.

3. Use a narrow satin stitch to create the features of the cat's face and whiskers. I used brown thread.

4. Remove the stabilizer from the back of the block. A hemostat or tweezers will make this task much easier.

Assembling and Quilting

1. From the yellow print border fabric, cut three strips 2½" by the width of the fabric. Trim two of the strips to 40" long. From the remaining strip, cut two pieces, 2½" x 16".

2. Using a ½"-wide seam, sew the two long border strips to the sides of the table runner. Press the seams toward the borders. Sew the short border strips to the ends of the table runner in the same manner.

3. Cut a piece of batting and backing fabric each 18" x 45". Layer the table runner, batting, and backing fabric and pin baste the layers together.

4. Quilt the table runner by machine or by hand. In the large area of blue background fabric, I quilted leafy vines using green thread and echo quilted around them with red thread. The other areas were mostly echo quilted. In the border, I stitched a series of three parallel straight lines.

Finishing

1. Use a ruler and rotary cutter to square up the table runner to approximately 14½" by 42".

2. From the dark blue print, cut three binding strips, 3" x 42". Sew the strips together end to end and attach the binding to the table runner, following the directions on page 18.

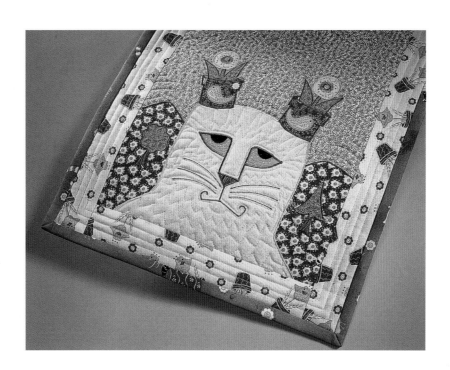

Flowering Feline
Enlarge pattern 110% for quilt block and glass vase.
Enlarge 137% for table runner.

Will Mew Marry Me?
Quilt Block

JUNE

I'm sure the answer will be "Yes!" for this romantic. The techniques used to create this block include appliqué, painting, quilting, hand embroidery, and beading. Metallic paints and gold beads add shine and pizzazz, as does the gold metallic thread used for satin-stitch appliqué. Green metallic paint around the champagne glasses adds a further bit of glitz while helping to define the shapes. The hearts on the cat are painted, too, which is quicker than stitching them. For a three-dimensional touch, I added a bit of tulle for a veil, which was gathered and stitched on by hand and finished with purchased ribbon flowers along the gathered edge.

Materials

Yardage is based on 42"-wide fabric.

- 10" square of print fabric for background
- 8" x 10" scrap of taupe fabric for cat
- Scraps of cream, green, pink, and black fabrics for appliqué details
- ¼ yard of pink print for binding
- 10" square of backing fabric
- 10" square of low-loft cotton batting
- ½ yard of Steam-A-Seam 2 fusible web
- ⅜ yard of stabilizer
- Tracing paper or acetate
- Black permanent pen
- Threads for machine embroidery in desired colors
- Transparent thread
- Bobbin thread
- Jacquard Lumiere paints in Halo Pink Gold, Metallic Olive Green, and Bright Gold
- Small heart stamp (optional)
- Paintbrush: #0 liner
- 12 gold seed beads, beading thread, and beading needle
- 4" x 6" scrap of tulle
- 12" of narrow white silk ribbon or embroidery floss and embroidery needle
- 2 cream and 1 pink purchased ribbon flowers
- 2 small plastic curtain rings

Preparation

Read the "Fusible Appliqué" section on page 10 before beginning.

1. Enlarge the Will Mew Marry Me? pattern (page 58) 110% on a photocopier.
2. Prepare an overlay or positioning guide by tracing the entire enlarged design onto acetate or tracing paper with a permanent pen.

3. Turn the overlay to the wrong side and trace each individual appliqué pattern piece (they'll be in reverse) onto one side of the paper layer of the Steam-A-Seam 2 fusible web. The shapes are numbered in the order that they should be appliquéd. Cut around the shapes on the fusible web, leaving a ⅛" to ¼" allowance around the drawn line.

4. Starting with piece 1, remove the paper layer from the opposite side of the drawn shape and discard. Hand press the fusible web with the pattern onto the back of the fabric you want to use for that appliqué shape. Do not iron in place yet.

5. Cut out the fabric, following the drawn lines on the paper layer, and leaving the paper layer intact. Set aside. Repeat steps 4 and 5 for each shape to be appliquéd.

6. Place the acetate or tissue-paper overlay on the 10" print background square, referring to "Fusible Appliqué." The print fabric will be the base for the other fabrics.

7. Working in numerical order, remove the paper layer from each shape and position it in place before ironing down permanently. Overlap where necessary.

8. With an iron, press all shapes into position, following the manufacturer's instructions for the fusible web.

Appliqué and Embellishment

1. Iron or pin stabilizer to the back of the block.

2. Use a machine satin stitch or blanket stitch, or hand stitch around each shape in the desired thread colors. I used gold metallic thread to satin stitch the champagne glasses. Working from the background to the foreground, continue until all shapes have been appliquéd.

3. Use a narrow satin stitch to create the cat's mouth and whiskers. I used dark gray thread for the mouth and light gray thread for the whiskers.

4. Paint the stripes on the hatband and the detail in the champagne glasses with the pink-gold paint.

5. Paint bright gold hearts on the cat and then outline them with the pink-gold paint after the bright gold paint has dried.

Note: Gold hearts may be applied using a small heart-shaped stamp and gold paint if desired.

6. Paint a narrow line of metallic green paint around the champagne glasses to define the shapes.

7. Remove the stabilizer from the back of the block. A hemostat or tweezers will make this task much easier.

8. Layer the quilt block with the 10" squares of batting and backing fabric. Pin all three layers together with the block right side up on top, the batting in the middle, and the backing fabric on the bottom, right side down.

9. Quilt the layers together by machine or by hand. I stipple quilted the background and used free-motion straight stitching in an up-and-down pattern to create a fur texture for the cat. I also outline quilted each of the painted hearts.

Finishing

1. Thread a needle with a 12"-long piece of silk ribbon or embroidery floss and knot one end. Insert the needle from the back of the quilt at point A next to the cat's ear. Pull the ribbon to the front.

2. Fold the tulle in half lengthwise and insert the needle into the top edge of the tulle, gathering it by hand with the ribbon.

3. Insert the needle into point B and pull the ribbon to the back of the block. Adjust the gathers and then anchor the tulle into position at three or four points with French knots (see page 14).

4. Using transparent thread, hand sew the flowers to the gathered edge of the veil.

5. Use a ruler and rotary cutter to trim the block to 9" x 9".

6. Cut a 3" x 42" strip of pink print for binding and attach it, following the directions on page 18.

7. Sew the curtain rings to the back of the block, aligning them to correspond with the cup hooks on the plaque.

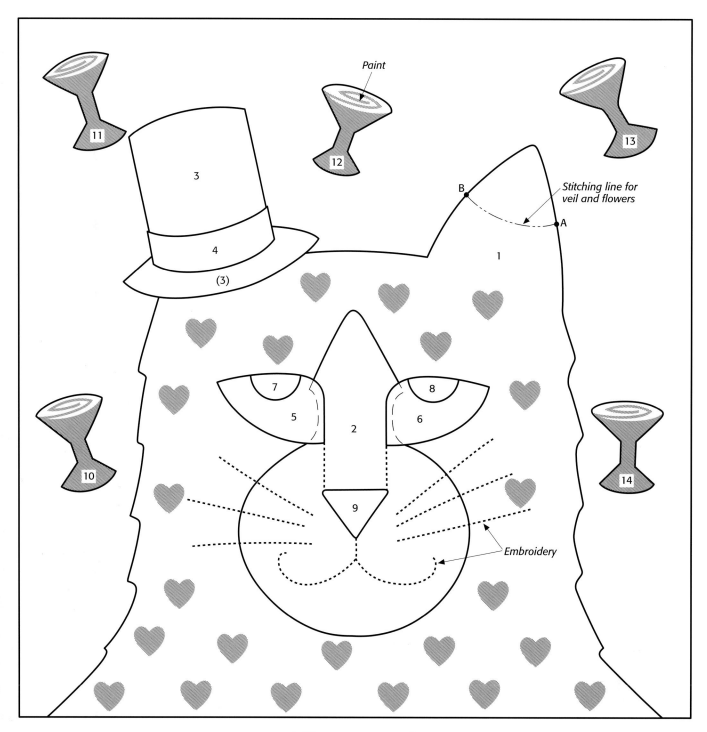

Will Mew Marry Me?
Enlarge pattern 110%.

Note: Piece 3 is one piece with the hat band (piece 4) appliquéd on top of it.

Yankee Doodle Tabby
Quilt Block

JULY

This patriotic puss knows how to celebrate. It's stars and stripes fur-ever! Fabric choices, from the down-home ticking stripes and gingham checks to the navy blue batik stars, set the mood for this all-star salute. Top the whole thing off with some razzle-dazzle effects, using red and silver metallic threads for satin stitching and Holoshimmer thread for quilting, and you'll be ready for the festivities!

Materials

Yardage is based on 42"-wide fabric.

- 10" square of dark blue star print for background
- 8" x 10" scrap of brown print for cat
- Scraps of red-and-white ticking, red, cream, light blue, and black fabrics for appliqué details
- ¼ yard of red-and-white check for binding
- 10" square of backing fabric
- 10" square of low-loft cotton batting
- ½ yard of Steam-A-Seam 2 fusible web
- ⅜ yard of stabilizer
- Tracing paper or acetate
- Black permanent pen
- Threads for machine embroidery in desired colors
- Bobbin thread
- 2 small plastic curtain rings

Preparation

Read the "Fusible Appliqué" section on page 10 before beginning.

1. Enlarge the Yankee Doodle Tabby pattern (page 62) 110% on a photocopier.
2. Prepare an overlay or positioning guide by tracing the entire enlarged design onto acetate or tracing paper with a permanent pen.
3. Turn the overlay to the wrong side and trace each individual appliqué pattern piece (they'll be in reverse) onto one side of the paper layer of the Steam-A-Seam 2 fusible web. The shapes are numbered in the order that they should be appliquéd. Cut around the shapes on the fusible web, leaving a ⅛" to ¼" allowance around the drawn line.
4. Starting with piece 1, remove the paper layer from the opposite side of the drawn shape and discard. Hand press the fusible web with the pattern onto the back of the fabric you want to use for that appliqué shape. Do not iron in place yet.
5. Cut out the fabric, following the drawn lines on the paper layer and leaving the paper layer intact. Set aside. Repeat steps 4 and 5 for each shape to be appliquéd.
6. Place the acetate or tissue-paper overlay on the 10" dark blue star print background square, referring to "Fusible Appliqué." The dark blue fabric will be the base for the other fabrics.

7. Working in numerical order, remove the paper layer from each shape and position it in place before ironing down permanently. Overlap where necessary.

8. With an iron, press all shapes into position, following the manufacturer's instructions for the fusible web.

Appliqué

1. Iron or pin stabilizer to the back of the block.

2. Use a machine satin stitch or blanket stitch, or hand stitch around each shape in the desired thread colors. I used red metallic thread to satin stitch the stars and tan thread to satin stitch the cat's paws, eyes, nose, and tummy. Working from the background to the foreground, continue until all shapes have been appliquéd.

3. Use a narrow satin stitch to create the cat's mouth and whiskers and to make the wands of the star sparklers the cat is holding. I used tan thread for the facial details and silver metallic thread to create the wands.

4. Remove the stabilizer from the back of the block. A hemostat or tweezers will make this task much easier.

5. Layer the quilt block with the 10" squares of batting and backing fabric. Pin all three layers together with the block right side up on top, the batting in the middle, and the backing fabric on the bottom, right side down.

6. Quilt the layers together by machine or by hand. I quilted the blue background in a loose stippling style using Holoshimmer thread, and the centers of the stars in a free-motion swirl with red metallic thread. Straight-stitch the cream colored areas of the cat and the stripes in the ticking fabric in the background. To add texture to the cat, use a thread that is lighter than the appliqué and stitch with an up-and-down motion to create zigzag fur.

Finishing

1. Use a ruler and rotary cutter to trim the block to 9" x 9".

2. Cut a 3" x 42" strip of red-and-white check fabric for binding and attach it, following the directions on page 18.

3. Sew the curtain rings to the back of the block, aligning them to correspond with the cup hooks on the plaque.

Yankee Doodle Tabby
Enlarge pattern 110%.

Scuba-Duba Mew
Quilt Block

AUGUST

This diver thinks of everything. His fashionable fish hats protect his ears and act as camouflage, while his goggles improve his underwater vision. This summertime design would enhance a bathroom, sunroom, pool house, or child's room, either as a wall hanging of the quilt block or enlarged to use on a painted floorcloth. Directions for the floorcloth begin on page 66.

Materials

Yardage is based on 42"-wide fabric.

- 10" square of light blue fabric for background
- 6" x 10" scrap of light brown print for cat
- 5" x 8" scrap of multicolored stripe for water
- Scraps of blue green, light green, black, and brown for appliqué details
- ¼ yard of turquoise print for goggles and binding
- 10" square of backing fabric
- 10" square of low-loft cotton batting
- ½ yard of Steam-A-Seam 2 fusible web
- ⅜ yard of stabilizer
- Tracing paper or acetate
- Black permanent pen
- Threads for machine embroidery in desired colors
- Bobbin thread
- Jacquard Lumiere paint in Gold
- Paintbrush: round #3
- 2 small plastic curtain rings

Preparation

Read the "Fusible Appliqué" section on page 10 before beginning.

1. Enlarge the Scuba-Duba Mew pattern (page 68) 110% on a photocopier.
2. Prepare an overlay or positioning guide by tracing the entire enlarged design onto acetate or tracing paper with a permanent pen.
3. Turn the overlay to the wrong side and trace each individual appliqué pattern piece (they'll be in reverse) onto one side of the paper layer of the Steam-A-Seam 2 fusible web. The shapes are numbered in the order that they should be appliquéd. Cut around the shapes on the fusible web, leaving a ⅛" to ¼" allowance around the drawn line.
4. Starting with piece 1, remove the paper layer from the opposite side of the drawn shape and discard. Hand press the fusible web with the pattern onto the back of the fabric you want to use for that appliqué shape. Do not iron in place yet.
5. Cut out the fabric, following the drawn lines on the paper layer and leaving the paper layer intact. Set aside. Repeat steps 4 and 5 for each shape to be appliquéd.
6. Place the acetate or tissue-paper overlay on the 10" light blue background square, referring to "Fusible Appliqué." The fabric will be the base for the other fabrics.

7. Working in numerical order, remove the paper layer from each shape and position it in place before ironing down permanently. Overlap where necessary.

8. With an iron, press all shapes into position, following the manufacturer's instructions for the fusible web.

Appliqué and Embellishment

1. Iron or pin stabilizer to the back of the block.

2. Use a machine satin stitch or blanket stitch, or hand stitch around each shape in the desired thread colors. Working from the background to the foreground, continue until all shapes have been appliquéd.

3. Use a narrow satin stitch to create the cat's mouth and whiskers. I used brown thread.

4. Remove the stabilizer from the back of the block. A hemostat or tweezers will make this task much easier.

5. Layer the quilt block with the 10" squares of batting and backing fabric. Pin all three layers together with the block right side up on top, the batting in the middle, and the backing fabric on the bottom, right side down.

6. Quilt the layers together by machine or by hand. I used echo quilting in the sky around the fish shapes. For the water I used Sulky's Holoshimmer thread, following the wavy lines in the striped fabric. I stitched the cat in free-motion straight stitches in an up-and-down pattern to create fur texture. For the fish, I quilted rows of scallop shapes to make scales and straight lines on the fins and tails.

7. Dilute the gold paint with water to create a liquid consistency and apply it with the round brush to the fish to add shimmer on the scales and to accent the tails and fins.

8. Allow the paint to dry for 24 hours before heat-setting it according to the manufacturer's directions.

Finishing

1. Use a ruler and rotary cutter to trim the block to 9" x 9".

2. Cut a 3" x 42" strip of turquoise print fabric for binding and attach it, following the directions on page 18.

3. Sew the curtain rings to the back of the block, aligning them to correspond with the cup hooks on the plaque.

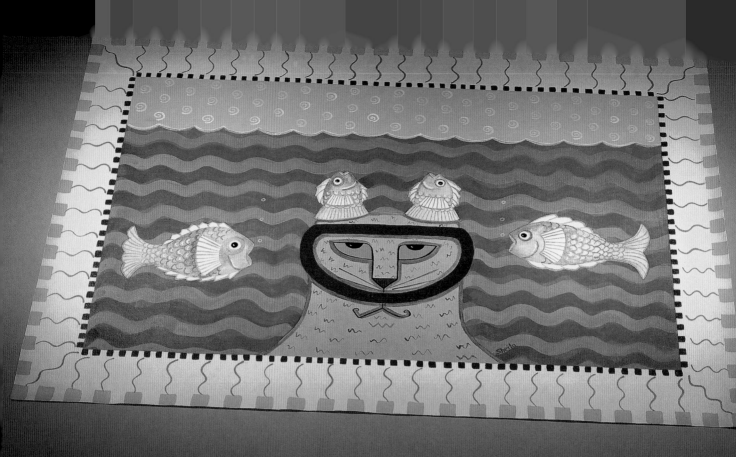

Scuba-Duba Mew Painted Floorcloth

🌀 *This floorcloth was great fun to paint and it features the use of glazes to add depth and detail. Two additional fish patterns are included for this project, which measures 24" x 36".*

Materials

- 24" x 36" piece of Fredrix preprimed or other canvas

- Gesso

- Delta Ceramcoat acrylic paints in Blue Heaven, Azure Blue, Wedgwood Green, Crocus Yellow, Trail Tan, Opaque Red, Opaque Blue, White, Spice Brown, Tomato Spice, and Black

- Delta Ceramcoat glaze

- Delta Ceramcoat satin indoor varnish

- Paintbrushes: ¾" and 1" wash brushes; size #0, #2, #4, and #8 round brushes; #10 shader; #4 flat brush; 2" gesso brush

- Pencil

- Ruler

- Graphite paper or light table

- Small containers for mixing paints and glazes

- 24" x 36" of nonskid rug mat

Preparation

1. Cut the preprimed canvas to 24" x 36" or prepare raw canvas as directed in "Prepping Canvas" on page 21.
2. Coat the edges of the primed canvas with gesso and let dry.
3. Enlarge the Scuba-Duba Mew pattern (page 68) 163% on a photocopier. The cat should be 11½" tall.
4. Use a ruler to draw a border 3" inside all four sides of the canvas.
5. Transfer the cat design to the inner rectangle of the canvas using graphite paper or a light table, referring to "Transferring Patterns" on page 22. In addition, transfer the fish patterns (page 69) to the canvas. The fish are full-size and do not need to be enlarged.

Painting the Floorcloth

1. Paint the sky with Blue Heaven paint, using the 1" brush.
2. Paint the water area Azure Blue, using the 1" brush. The wavy stripes will be added later.
3. Paint the 3"-wide border yellow, using the 1" brush.
4. Using the shader brush, paint the cat's eyes green and the cat's body tan.
5. Using the #4 flat brush, paint the goggles Opaque Red and paint all four fish yellow.

Note: Glazes of semitransparent color are used to add color and contrast to the floor cloth. There is no exact formula for mixing glazes. Begin by mixing one part paint to two parts glaze base and one part water. The consistency should be liquid. Add more paint if the glaze is too faint. Add more glaze base if the glaze is too opaque. Always test the glaze on a scrap of paper or canvas before applying to the floor cloth.

6. Mix Opaque Blue, glaze base, and water to create a darker glaze for the water background. Apply the glaze in wavy lines over the water background, using the 1" brush. Save the leftover glaze to add the wavy lines in the border later.

7. Mix a lighter blue glaze for the water background by adding white to the glaze made in step 6 and apply it in wavy lines, using the ¾" brush.
8. Mix a white glaze and outline the top of the waves, using the #8 round brush. Use the same white glaze to paint swirls in the sky and bubbles coming from the mouths of the swimming fish, using the #4 round brush.
9. Paint the cat's nose brown with the #2 round brush.
10. Paint the cat's pupils black and outline the cat's eyes, nose, and mouth in black with the #0 round brush.
11. Mix a brown glaze and use it to create shadow and dimension to the design with the #8 round brush. Use the brown glaze around the outline of the cat, under the fish, on the cat's ears, on the inside of the mask, and on the face details. Use the same glaze to paint wavy lines of texture and the whiskers on the cat with the #0 round brush.
12. Mix a glaze of Tomato Spice and glazing liquid to paint the scales and fins of all of the fish, using the #8 and #0 round brushes.
13. Add yellow highlights to the fish with the #0 round brush. Paint the fish's eyes black with the #0 round brush.
14. Paint red checks around the inner border, using the #4 flat brush.
15. Paint Blue Heaven checks around the outer border, using the ¾" wash brush. Using the #0 round brush, paint wavy lines in the border with the remaining Opaque Blue glaze.
16. Paint a 2"-wide yellow border around the edges of the underside of the floorcloth.

Finishing

1. Apply five or six coats of the interior varnish with the 2" gesso brush to the top of the floorcloth, allowing each coat to dry thoroughly between applications.
2. Apply two or three coats of the varnish to the back border, again allowing the varnish to dry thoroughly between coats.
3. Trim the nonskid mat so it is slightly smaller than the floorcloth, or apply a coat of no-skid product to the back of the floorcloth to prevent it from slipping when in use.

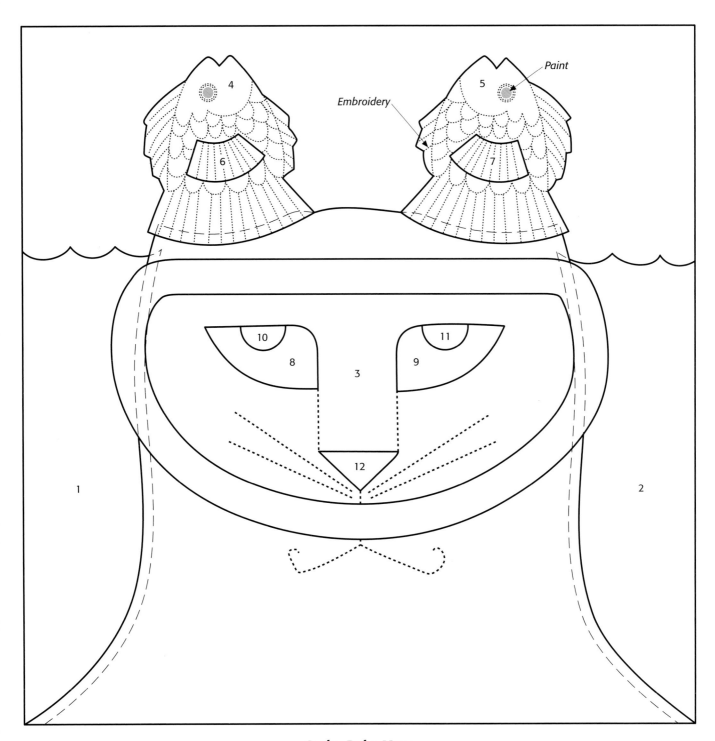

Scuba-Duba Mew
Enlarge pattern 110% for quilt block.
Enlarge pattern 163% for floorcloth.

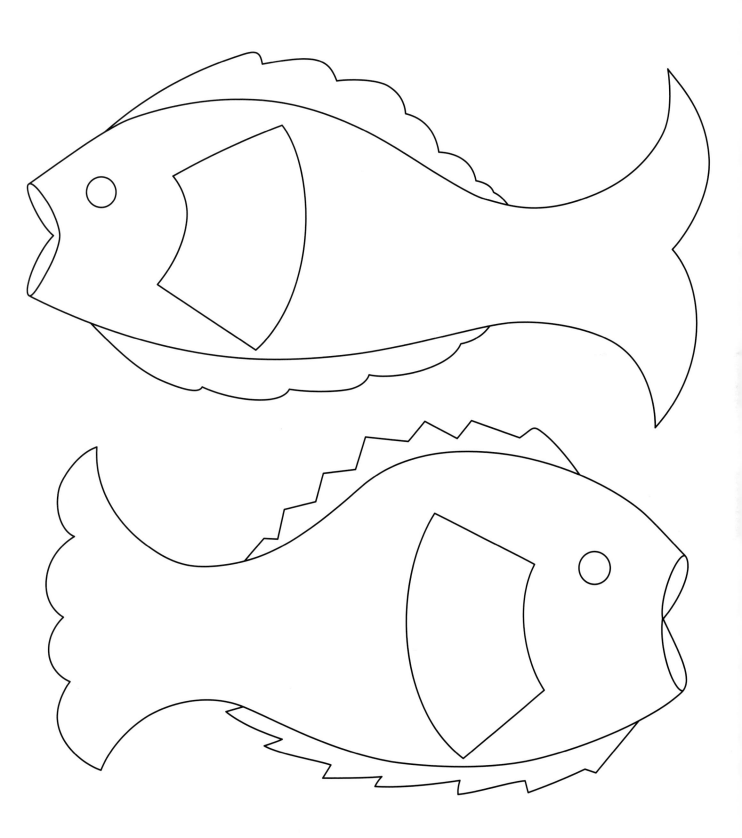

Scuba-Duba Mew Floorcloth
Patterns are full-size.

SEPTEMBER

Leafy Lion
Quilt Block

This royal fellow is caught in a swirl of fall colors. It seemed only fitting that the leaves should be touched with gold. Bright gold paint applied to the leaves as a wash and to the lion's fur enhances his regal appearance. To complete the effect, paint gold stripes on the binding after it is stitched in place.

Materials

Yardage is based on 42"-wide fabric.

- 10" square of light blue fabric for background
- 7" x 10" scrap of brown fabric for lion and nose
- 5"square of light tan for lion's face
- Scraps of yellow, red, green, orange, and black for appliqué details
- ¼ yard of green fabric for binding
- 10" square of backing fabric
- 10" square of low-loft cotton batting
- ½ yard of Steam-A-Seam 2 fusible web
- ⅜ yard of stabilizer
- Tracing paper or acetate
- Black permanent pen
- Threads for machine embroidery in desired colors
- Bobbin thread
- Jacquard Lumiere paint in Bright Gold
- Paintbrush: #1 round
- 2 small plastic curtain rings

Preparation

Read the "Fusible Appliqué" section on page 10 before beginning.

1. Enlarge the Leafy Lion pattern (page 73) 110% on a photocopier.
2. Prepare an overlay or positioning guide by tracing the entire enlarged design onto acetate or tracing paper with a permanent pen.
3. Turn the overlay to the wrong side and trace each individual appliqué pattern piece (they'll be in reverse) onto one side of the paper layer of the Steam-A-Seam 2 fusible web. The shapes are numbered in the order that they should be appliquéd. Cut around the shapes on the fusible web, leaving a ⅛" to ¼" allowance around the drawn line.
4. Starting with piece 1, remove the paper layer from the opposite side of the drawn shape and discard. Hand press the fusible web with the pattern onto the back of the fabric you want to use for that appliqué shape. Do not iron in place yet.
5. Cut out the fabric, following the drawn lines on the paper layer and leaving the paper layer intact. Set aside. Repeat steps 4 and 5 for each shape to be appliquéd.
6. Place the acetate or tissue-paper overlay on the 10" light blue background square, referring to "Fusible Appliqué." The blue fabric will be the base for the other fabrics.

7. Working in numerical order, remove the paper layer from each shape and position it in place before ironing down permanently. Overlap where necessary.

8. With an iron, press all shapes into position, following the manufacturer's instructions for the fusible web.

Appliqué and Embellishment

1. Iron or pin stabilizer to the back of the block.

2. Use a machine satin stitch or blanket stitch, or hand stitch around each shape in the desired thread colors. Working from the background to the foreground, continue until all shapes have been appliquéd.

3. Use a narrow satin stitch to create the lion's mouth and whiskers. I used brown thread.

4. Remove the stabilizer from the back of the block. A hemostat or tweezers will make this task much easier.

5. Layer the quilt block with the 10" squares of batting and backing fabric. Pin all three layers together with the block right side up on top, the batting in the middle, and the backing fabric on the bottom, right side down.

6. Quilt the layers together by machine or by hand. I outline quilted the lion and leaves, and then stipple quilted in the remaining background area. You can use the lines on the leaf patterns to free-motion quilt veins in the leaves; to add interest, curl the ends of the veins in the green leaves. I quilted the lion with an up-and-down pattern to create contrast and a zigzag texture.

Finishing

1. Use a ruler and rotary cutter to trim the block to 9" x 9".

2. Cut a 3" x 42" strip of green fabric for binding and attach it, following the directions on page 18.

3. Dilute a small amount of the gold paint with water to a liquid consistency and apply with the brush as a wash on the leaves and lines on the lion's fur.

4. Using full-strength paint, paint gold stripes on the binding. Heat-set the paint as directed by the manufacturer.

5. Sew the curtain rings to the back of the block, aligning them to correspond with the cup hooks on the plaque.

Leafy Lion
Enlarge pattern 110%.

OCTOBER

Boo to Mew
Quilt Block

You may be afraid to meet this cat in an alley, but he's really quite harmless. He's simply dressed for the occasion! This quilt-block design features gold paint and shimmering threads to add sparkle and a glow to the spooky scene. Small green bugle beads are used as stems on the pumpkin hats, and silver bugle beads create cat's fangs. The jack-o'-lantern faces were painted black, and gold dots highlight the eyes.

This design also works quite nicely stitched in felt for a purse or candy tote. Directions for that project begin on page 79.

Materials

Yardage is based on 42"-wide fabric.

- 10" square of royal blue fabric for background
- 8" x 10" scrap of black for cat and eyes
- Scraps of orange, yellow, gray, and green fabrics for appliqué details
- ¼ yard of black-and-white print for binding
- 10" square of backing fabric
- 10" square of low-loft cotton batting
- ½ yard of Steam-A-Seam 2 fusible web
- ⅜ yard of stabilizer
- Tracing paper or acetate
- Black permanent pen
- Threads for machine embroidery in desired colors
- Bobbin thread
- 2 green and 2 silver bugle beads, beading thread, and beading needle
- Jacquard Neopaque paint in Black
- Jacquard Lumiere paints in Bright Gold and Super Copper
- Paintbrush: #0 round
- 2 small plastic curtain rings

Preparation

Read the "Fusible Appliqué" section on page 10 before beginning.

1. Enlarge the Boo to Mew pattern (page 80) 110% on a photocopier.

2. Prepare an overlay or positioning guide by tracing the entire enlarged design onto acetate or tissue paper with a permanent pen.

3. Turn the overlay to the wrong side and trace each individual appliqué pattern piece (they'll be in reverse) onto one side of the paper layer of the Steam-A-Seam 2 fusible web. The shapes are numbered in the order that they should be appliquéd. Cut around the shapes on the fusible web, leaving a ⅛" to ¼" allowance around the drawn line.

4. Starting with piece 1, remove the paper layer from the opposite side of the drawn shape and discard. Hand press the fusible web with the pattern onto the back of the fabric you want to use for that appliqué shape. Do not iron in place yet.

5. Cut out the fabric, following the drawn lines on the paper layer and leaving the paper layer intact. Set aside. Repeat steps 4 and 5 for each shape to be appliquéd.

6. Place the acetate or tissue-paper overlay on the 10" royal blue background square, referring to "Fusible Appliqué." The blue fabric will be the base for the other fabrics.

7. Working in numerical order, remove the paper layer from each shape and position it in place before ironing down permanently. Overlap where necessary.
8. With an iron, press all shapes into position, following the manufacturer's instructions for the fusible web.

Appliqué and Embellishment

1. Iron or pin stabilizer to the back of the block.
2. Use a machine satin stitch or blanket stitch, or hand stitch around each shape in the desired thread colors. Working from the background to the foreground, continue until all shapes have been appliquéd.
3. Use a narrow satin stitch to create the cat's mouth and whiskers. I used gray thread.
4. Remove the stabilizer from the back of the block. A hemostat or tweezers will make this task much easier.
5. Layer the quilt block with the 10" squares of batting and backing fabric. Pin all three layers together with the block right side up on top, the batting in the middle, and the backing fabric on the bottom, right side down.
6. Paint the facial features on the pumpkin hats with black paint, using the #0 brush.

7. Paint the yellow stars with touches of gold paint.
8. Paint the moon with copper paint diluted with water to a liquid consistency.
9. Heat-set paints according to the manufacturer's directions.
10. Quilt the layers together by machine or by hand. I used orange Holoshimmer thread to stipple quilt in the royal blue background for shiny color contrast. I used the same thread to echo quilt the moon, the pumpkin hats, and the stars. For the cat, I used black metallic thread to quilt in an up-and-down pattern to make zigzag lines that simulate the look of fur. The eyes are echo quilted with close lines of stitching.
11. Using the beading needle and beading thread, hand sew the green bugle beads to the tops of the pumpkins to make stems. Sew the silver bugle beads below the cat's mouth to create the fangs.

Finishing

1. Use a ruler and rotary cutter to trim the block to 9" x 9".
2. Cut a 3" x 42" strip of black-and-white print for the binding and attach it, following the directions on page 18. I painted gold dots in the center of each star in the binding. If you have a different type of print, you may want to do a different type of paint treatment. If you do paint the binding, remember to heat-set the paint.
3. Sew the curtain rings to the back of the block, aligning them to correspond with the cup hooks on the plaque.

Boo to Mew Felt Purse

Felt is so easy to use and has such a nice, warm look to it that I couldn't resist stitching the Boo to Mew design as a felt bag. Machine blanket stitching outlines the different shapes, but if you enjoy hand embroidery, you can easily do the same stitch by hand. Just as on the quilt block, I used orange Holoshimmer thread to add sparkle to the design. I also added two more appliquéd stars to fill in the background area. Instead of painting pumpkin faces on felt, I stitched black seed beads in place to make the jack-o'-lantern faces. To add interest and a bit of whimsy to the back of the purse, I stitched a large star with a swirling center. You can follow this lead or stitch your own unique design.

Materials

Yardage is based on 42"-wide fabric.

- Wool-blend felt from National Nonwovens:

  Two 10" squares of Purple Sage felt for purse

  One 8" square of Black felt for cat and cat's eyes

  Scraps of orange, gray, and yellow felt for pumpkins, moon, cat's nose, cat's eyes, and stars

- ⅜ yard of fabric for lining
- ½ yard of Steam-A-Seam 2 fusible web
- Two 10" squares of fusible interfacing
- Tracing paper or acetate
- Black permanent pen
- Threads for machine embroidery in desired colors
- Bobbin thread
- 1⅛ yards of ¼"-diameter black cording for purse strap
- Seam sealant, such as Fray Block or Fray Check
- ½"-diameter button
- 3" of ³⁄₁₆"-wide black velveteen ribbon for purse closure
- 16 black seed beads, 2 green and 2 silver bugle beads, beading thread, and beading needle

Preparation

Read the "Fusible Appliqué" section on page 10 before beginning.

1. Trim the two pieces of purple felt to 10" x 10" for purse front and back.
2. Iron a 10" square of fusible interfacing onto the wrong side of each purple felt square to stabilize them for stitching.
3. Enlarge the Boo to Mew pattern (page 80) 110% on a photocopier.
4. Prepare an overlay or positioning guide by tracing the entire enlarged design onto acetate or tracing paper with a permanent pen.
5. Turn the overlay to the wrong side and trace each individual appliqué pattern piece (they'll be in reverse) onto one side of the paper layer of the Steam-A-Seam 2 fusible web. The shapes are numbered in the order that they should be appliquéd. Cut around the shapes on the fusible web, leaving a ⅛" to ¼" allowance around the drawn line.
6. Starting with piece 1, remove the paper layer from the opposite side of the drawn shape and discard. Hand press the fusible web with the pattern onto the back of the felt you want to use for that appliqué shape. Do not iron in place yet.
7. Cut out the felt, following the drawn lines on the paper layer and leaving the paper layer intact. Set aside. Repeat steps 4 and 5 for each shape to be appliquéd.
8. Place the acetate or tissue-paper overlay on the 10" purple background square, referring to "Fusible Appliqué."

9. Working in numerical order, remove the paper layer from each shape and position it in place before ironing down permanently. Overlap where necessary.
10. With an iron, press all shapes into position, following the manufacturer's instructions for the fusible web.

Appliqué and Embellishment

1. Appliqué the cat, stars, and moon with a blanket stitch by machine or by hand.
2. Appliqué the cat's eyes and nose and outline the mouth with a narrow satin stitch. I used gray thread.
3. Embellish the cat with free-motion straight stitching in an up-and-down pattern to simulate the look of fur. I used black thread.
4. Create whiskers with lines of straight stitching, curving the end of each line upward so the whiskers are curled. I used gray thread.
5. Echo stitch in the background around the cat and stars. I used orange Holoshimmer thread. Using the same thread, I stitched swirls in the stars and lines of echo quilting in the cat's eyes and in the moon.
6. Using the beading needle and beading thread, hand sew the green bugle beads to the tops of the pumpkins for stems, and the silver bugle beads below the cat's mouth for fangs. Also sew the black seed beads to the pumpkins to create the facial features.
7. If desired, free-motion stitch a large star with a swirl in the center on the other prepared felt piece for the back of the purse.

Purse Assembly

1. With right sides facing, sew the front and back of the purse together with a ½" seam allowance. Sew only three sides of the purse, making sure to leave the top edge open.
2. Cut two pieces of lining fabric 10" x 10". With right sides facing, sew the front and back linings together along three sides, again using a ½" seam. Leave a 3" opening in one of the side seams for turning once the purse is assembled.
3. Fold the 3"-long piece of ribbon in half to form a loop for the button closure. Pin the ribbon to the top edge of the purse back, aligning the raw edges of the ribbon with the raw edge of the purse. The loop will be facing toward the bottom of the purse. Hand or machine baste in place.
4. Pin the lining to the purse, right sides together, and stitch them together along the top edges of the purse, using a ½" seam. Turn the purse right side out through the opening in the side of the lining. Sew the opening closed by hand or machine and slip the lining in position inside the purse.
5. Sew the button to the front of the purse, lining it up with the ribbon loop to create the closure.
6. Cut cording to desired length, depending on whether the purse will be a shoulder bag or hand bag. The purse shown has a 39"-long strap, including 1½" allowances on each end where it is sewn in place. Hand sew the cording in place on the inside of each side of the purse, stitching through the lining and the felt to secure it. Cover the ends of the cording with the seam sealant to prevent fraying.

Boo to Mew
Enlarge pattern 110%.

Note: Two stars were added for the felt purse.

Tom and Two Turkeys
Quilt Block

NOVEMBER

This tomcat has so much to be thankful for and it shows in his look of contentment. To spice up the holiday look, add a touch of gold paint to embellish the block background and the turkeys. Glass seed beads add color and sparkle to the turkeys, too.

To really set the mood for your next Thanksgiving feast, you might want to make the painted wooden tray shown on page 84. If you use the tray to serve food with any moisture in it, cover the tray with clear plastic first.

Materials

Yardage is based on 42"-wide fabric.

- 10" square of green print for background
- 8" x 10" scrap of tan check for cat
- Scraps of yellow, black, and brown for appliqué details
- ¼ yard of red print for binding
- 10" square of backing fabric
- 10" square of low-loft cotton batting
- ½ yard of Steam-A-Seam 2 fusible web
- ⅜ yard of stabilizer
- Tracing paper or acetate
- Black permanent pen
- Threads for machine embroidery in desired colors
- Bobbin thread
- Jacquard Lumiere paint in Gold
- Paintbrush: #0 round
- 2 gold and 16 red seed beads, 2 red bugle beads, beading thread, and beading needle
- 2 small plastic curtain rings

Preparation

Read the "Fusible Appliqué" section on page 10 before beginning.

1. Enlarge the Tom and Two Turkeys pattern (page 87) 110% on a photocopier.
2. Prepare an overlay or positioning guide by tracing the entire enlarged design onto acetate or tracing paper with a permanent pen.
3. Turn the overlay to the wrong side and trace each individual appliqué pattern piece (they'll be in reverse) onto one side of the paper layer of the Steam-A-Seam 2 fusible web. The shapes are numbered in the order that they should be appliquéd. Cut around the shapes on the fusible web, leaving a ⅛" to ¼" allowance around the drawn line.
4. Starting with piece 1, remove the paper layer from the opposite side of the drawn shape and discard. Hand press the fusible with the pattern onto the back of the fabric you want to use for that appliqué shape. Do not iron in place yet.
5. Cut out the fabric, following the drawn lines on the paper layer and leaving the paper layer intact. Set aside. Repeat steps 4 and 5 for each shape to be appliquéd.
6. Place the acetate or tissue-paper overlay on the 10" green print background square, referring to "Fusible Appliqué." The green fabric will be the base for the other fabrics.

7. Working in numerical order, remove the paper layer from each shape and position it in place before ironing down permanently. Overlap where necessary.

8. With an iron, press all shapes into position, following the manufacturer's instructions for the fusible web.

Appliqué and Embellishment

1. Iron or pin stabilizer to the back of the block.

2. Use a machine satin stitch or blanket stitch, or hand stitch around each shape in the desired thread colors. Working from the background to the foreground, continue until all shapes have been appliquéd.

3. Use a narrow satin stitch to create the cat's mouth and whiskers. I used brown thread.

4. Remove the stabilizer from the back of the block. A hemostat or tweezers will make this task much easier.

5. Layer the quilt block with the 10" squares of batting and backing fabric. Pin all three layers together with the block right side up on top, the batting in the middle, and the backing fabric on the bottom, right side down.

6. Quilt the layers together by machine or by hand. I quilted the background by following the lines in the green print. For the cat, I stitched straight lines in an up-and-down pattern to create fur texture.

7. Dilute the gold paint slightly with water to a liquid consistency and use the round brush to paint swirling lines in the green print background areas. Apply the same diluted gold paint to the turkeys to simulate the feathers, eyes, and beaks.

8. Using the beading needle and beading thread, hand stitch a gold seed bead onto each turkey for an eye. Sew the red seed beads to the turkey tail feathers and wings, and attach a red bugle bead to each turkey's waddle.

Finishing

1. Use a ruler and rotary cutter to trim the block to 9" x 9".

2. Cut a 3" x 42" strip of red print for the binding and attach it, following the directions on page 18.

3. Sew the curtain rings to the back of the block, aligning them to correspond with the cup hooks on the plaque.

Tom and Two Turkeys
Painted Wooden Tray

The contented kitty on this painted wooden tray looks ready for the feast. The stylized red flowers complete the look and are perfectly suited to the circular design. Cover the tray with clear platic wrap before using it to serve food that has any moisture in it.

Materials

- 13½" round wooden tray: Round Home Plate #23739 from Walnut Hollow Farm (see "Resources" on page 94)

- Gesso

- Delta Ceramcoat acrylic paints in Straw, Tomato Spice, Seminole Green, Wedgwood Green, Trail Tan, Spice Brown, Black, and White

- Paintbrushes: #2 round, #10 shader, #1 and #4 round, #18/0 liner, #2 flat, #4 flat, 1" flat wash brush

- Tracing paper

- Graphite paper

- Delta Ceramcoat interior satin varnish

- Fine sandpaper

Preparation

1. Lightly sand tray with fine sandpaper and remove the dust.
2. Apply one coat of gesso to the top, sides, and bottom of the tray. When gesso has dried, lightly sand the tray and remove the dust.
3. Enlarge the Tom and Two Turkeys pattern (page 87) 110% on a photocopier.
4. Measure and mark 2" from the edge of the tray all around to designate the border.
5. Trace the outer edges of the tray onto the tracing-paper pattern and cut along the traced edge to make a placement guide. Fold the guide in half and then fold in half again to find the center point of the circle. Place the tracing-paper circle over the enlarged photocopy pattern of the cat and trace the design onto the circle.
6. Center the traced pattern on the tray and slide a piece of graphite paper underneath the pattern, graphite side facing down. Using a pencil, draw over the pattern lines to transfer the designs to the tray.
7. With the placement guide still on the plate, mark the horizontal and vertical centers along the outer edges of the plate with light pencil marks.
8. Trace the flower motif onto tracing paper. Line up the motif at each of the four points marked along the edges of the tray and trace a flower onto the surface, using a pencil and graphite paper. Trace additional flower motifs in place, spacing them equal distances apart. On the tray shown, there are three flowers marked in each quadrant of the tray.

Painting the Tray

1. Paint the border, edges, and back of the tray yellow (Straw), using the 1" flat wash brush. Using the same paint, switch to the #2 brush and paint the cat's eyes.
2. Paint the background behind the cat Seminole Green, using the shader brush.
3. Paint the cat tan, using the #4 round brush.
4. Paint the turkeys brown, the wings tan, and the tail and head red, using the #1 brush.
5. Paint the stems and leaves of the flowers Wedgwood Green, using the #1 brush. Paint the veins and outlines of the leaves Seminole Green with slightly diluted paint and the #18/0 liner brush.
6. With red paint and the #2 round brush, paint the oval shapes of the flowers. With the same paint and the #1 brush, paint the dots around the leaves and flowers and the dotted inner border.
7. Paint the swirled lines in the flowers yellow, using the #18/0 liner brush.
8. Paint small swirls on the green background, using slightly diluted red paint and the #18/0 liner brush.
9. Paint the pupils of the cat's eyes and turkeys' eyes black, using the #18/0 liner brush.
10. Paint the cat's nose and the turkey bodies brown, using the #0 liner brush.
11. Dilute brown paint and use the #0 liner brush to paint the facial details of the cat.
12. Mix a small amount of tan with brown and dilute the mixture slightly to paint the lines in the cat's fur and the turkeys' wings. Use the #0 liner brush.
13. Dilute white paint and use it to paint dots on the turkeys and the highlight line along the top of the wings, using the #18/0 brush. Add a small dot of white to each pupil in the cat's eyes.
14. Dilute yellow paint to add small dots of color to the turkeys' tail feathers.
15. Mix a small amount of red and yellow paints to make an orange color and use it to paint the beaks of the turkeys with the #18/0 brush. Use the same brush and paint to add dots of orange on the turkey wings and a line of dots along the upper edge of the brown area of each turkey.
16. Add a small line of brown to the backs of the turkeys' heads with the same brush.
17. Create a checked effect on the edge of the tray by painting red strokes, spaced evenly, with the #4 flat brush.

Finishing

1. Using the 1" wash brush, apply a coat of satin or gloss interior varnish to the top, edges, and underside of the tray.
2. Allow the varnish to dry thoroughly and then sand lightly and remove any dust before applying two or three additional coats of varnish. Sand lightly between each coat.

Floral Motif
Pattern is full-size.

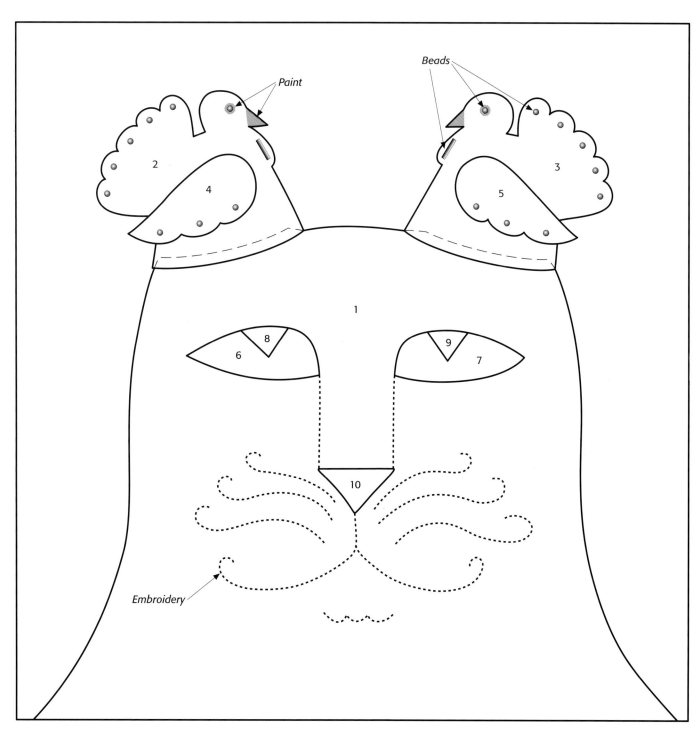

Tom and Two Turkeys
Enlarge pattern 110%.

DECEMBER

Tabby Tree-O
Quilt Block

This holiday trio wishes you "Hairy Holidays!" They're wearing their feelings on their ears, and who can resist their good cheer? Deck the trees with hand-embroidered gold stars and several colors of seed beads for ornaments. To add a festive mood to the background, try metallic or Holoshimmer thread and echo quilt around the Christmas-tree hats.

In addition to the festive quilt block, you'll find instructions, beginning on page 91, for painted glass ornaments or light catchers that feature this design as well as January's Cold as Mice design.

Materials

Yardage is based on 42"-wide fabric.

- 10" square of red print for background

- Scraps of black, white, gray, green, yellow, dark brown, cream, and light brown for cats, trees, and appliqué details

- ¼ yard of dark green fabric for binding

- 10" square of backing fabric

- 10" square of low-loft cotton batting

- ½ yard of Steam-A-Seam 2 fusible web

- ⅜ yard of stabilizer

- Tracing paper or acetate

- Black permanent pen

- Thread for machine embroidery in desired colors

- Bobbin thread

- About 60 seed beads in assorted colors, beading thread, and beading needle

- Gold metallic embroidery floss and embroidery needle

- 2 small plastic curtain rings

Preparation

Read the "Fusible Appliqué" section on page 10 before beginning.

1. Enlarge the Tabby Tree-O pattern (page 93) 110% on a photocopier.

2. Prepare an overlay or positioning guide by tracing the entire enlarged design onto acetate or tracing paper with a permanent pen.

3. Turn the overlay to the wrong side and trace each individual appliqué pattern piece (they'll be in reverse) onto one side of the paper layer of the Steam-A-Seam 2 fusible web. The shapes are numbered in the order that they should be appliquéd. Cut around the shapes on the fusible web, leaving a ⅛" to ¼" allowance around the drawn line.

4. Starting with piece 1, remove the paper layer from the opposite side of the drawn shape and discard. Hand press the fusible web with the pattern onto the back of the fabric you want to use for that appliqué shape. Do not iron in place yet.

5. Cut out the fabric, following the drawn lines on the paper layer and leaving the paper layer intact. Set aside. Repeat steps 4 and 5 for each shape to be appliquéd.

6. Place the acetate or tissue-paper overlay on the 10" red print background square, referring to "Fusible Appliqué." The red fabric will be the base for the other fabrics.

7. Working in numerical order, remove the paper layer from each shape and position it in place before ironing down permanently. Overlap where necessary.

8. With an iron, press all shapes into position, following the manufacturer's instructions for the fusible web.

Appliqué and Embellishment

1. Iron or pin stabilizer to the back of the block.

2. Use a machine satin stitch or blanket stitch, or hand stitch around each shape in the desired thread colors. Working from the background to the foreground, continue until all shapes have been appliquéd, except for the trees.

3. Use a narrow satin stitch to create the cats' mouths and whiskers. I used gray and brown threads.

4. Remove the stabilizer from the back of the block. A hemostat or tweezers will make this task much easier.

5. Layer the quilt block with the 10" squares of batting and backing fabric. Pin all three layers together with the block right side up on top, the batting in the middle, and the backing fabric on the bottom, right side down.

6. Quilt the layers together by machine or by hand. I echo quilted the background with green Holoshimmer thread. The cats were quilted mostly with free-motion straight stitching in an up-and-down pattern to create the texture of fur. For the white face of the black cat, I used echo quilting. For the trees, I used a similar technique as for the cats, stitching in an up-and-down pattern to simulate tree branches. Variegated green thread helps to give depth and texture to the trees.

7. Hand stitch the stars on the trees, using two or three strands of gold embroidery floss in simple cross-stitches as shown in the diagram on page 14.

8. Using the beading needle and beading thread, hand sew the colored seed beads on the trees.

Finishing

1. Use a ruler and rotary cutter to trim the block to 9" x 9".

2. Cut a 3" x 42" strip of dark green fabric for the binding and attach it, following the directions on page 18.

3. Sew the curtain rings to the back of the block, aligning them to correspond with the cup hooks on the plaque.

Tabby Tree-O and Cold as Mice
Painted Glass Ornaments

I reduced the patterns for the January and the December quilt blocks to create these whimsical painted glass tree ornaments, which can also double as sun catchers. The glass paints for these projects air-cure so they do not require baking. Adding a protective coating increases the durability of the paint.

Materials

- 5"-diameter round glass ornaments from Provo Craft (see "Resources" on page 94)

- Delta PermEnamel surface conditioner

- Delta PermEnamel glass paint in Liquid Lead Black

- Delta PermEnamel glass paint in White, Royal Blue, Kelly Green, Amber, Yellow, and Black

- Delta PermEnamel Gold Accent Liner (for Tabby Tree-O design only)

- Delta PermEnamel satin glaze

- Masking tape

- Metal tip for applying outline paints

- Paintbrushes: #0 round for small areas, #4 round for larger areas, #8 shader (a flat brush) for conditioner and glaze

- Fishing line, ribbon, or decorative cording for hanging ornaments

Preparation

1. Wash and dry the glass ornaments.
2. Apply surface conditioner to the glass, using the shader brush, and allow it to dry.

3. Reduce the patterns on a photocopier. The Cold as Mice pattern is on page 29; reduce it 59%. The Tabby Tree-O pattern is shown opposite; reduce it 63%.
4. Place the pattern underneath the prepared glass in the desired position and tape it in place with masking tape.

Painting the Ornaments

1. Outline the designs, using the black Liquid Lead with a metal tip placed on the end of the applicator bottle to aid in creating fine lines.
2. For the Tabby Tree-O design, add stars to the treetops using gold Accent Liner with a metal tip. Allow outlining paint to dry before adding paints.
3. Paint each shape, using the photograph for paint color reference. Amber paint was added to the center cat in the December design while the project was still wet.

Finishing

1. Allow the paints to dry thoroughly and then apply one coat of satin glaze, using the shader brush.
2. Attach fishing line, ribbon, or decorative cording to hang the ornaments from a Christmas tree or in a window.

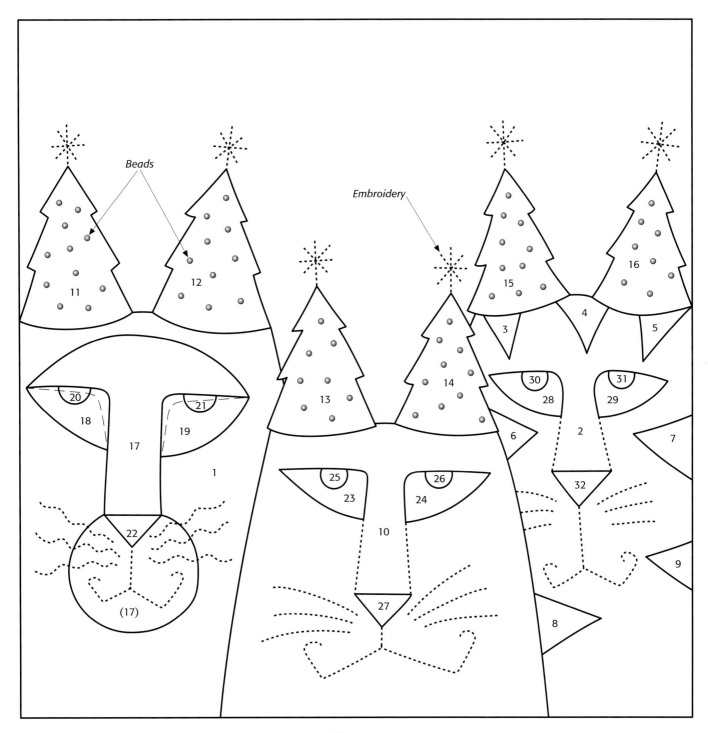

Tabby Tree-O
Enlarge pattern 110% for quilt block.
Reduce pattern 63% for glass ornament.

Note: Piece 17 includes entire white area of black cat.
Eyes and nose are appliquéd on top of the white.

Your local craft or fabric store is a good source for most of the products and tools needed to make the projects in this book. If you can't find a specific product, the list of manufacturers and suppliers below should help you locate exactly what you need.

A. C. Moore
500 University Ct.
Blackwood, NJ 08012
856-338-6700
*Paints and supplies, embellishments,
and other crafts supplies*

Bernina of America
3500 Thayer Ct.
Aurora, IL 60504
630-978-2500
www.berninausa.com
Sewing machines, needles

Clothworks Fabrics
A division of FASCO/Fabric Sales Company
6250 Stanley Ave. S.
Seattle, WA 98108
206-762-7886
www.clothworks-fabric.com
*Cotton fabrics designed by Sheila H. Rauen
and other designers*

Delta Technical Coatings, Inc.
2550 Pellissier Pl.
Whittier, CA 90601-1505
562-695-7969
www.deltacrafts.com
*Delta Ceramcoat paints and varnishes,
Delta PermEnamel paints and coatings*

Fiskars Brands, Inc.
7811 W. Stewart Ave.
Wausau, WI 54401
715-842-2091
Scissors, rotary cutters, cutting mats, rulers

Jacquard Products
Rupert, Gibbon, and Spider, Inc.
PO Box 425
Healdsburg, CA 95448
800-442-0455
www.jacquardproducts.com
Lumiere, Neopaque, and Textile paints

Jo-Ann Stores, Inc.
5555 Darrow Rd.
Hudson, OH 44236
330-656-2600
*Papier-mâché box, wooden tray, arts
and crafts supplies*

Loew-Cornell Brushes
563 Chestnut Ave.
Teaneck, NJ 07666-2490
201-836-7070
www.loew-cornell.com
Paintbrushes and accessories

Michael's Stores, Inc.
www.michaels.com
*Paints and supplies, embellishments,
and other craft supplies*

Resources

National Nonwovens
PO Box 150
Easthampton, MA 01027
800-333-3469
413-527-3445
www.nationalnonwovens.com
Wool-blend felts

Office Depot
2200 Old Germantown Rd.
Delray Beach, FL 88445
www.officedepot.com
Acetate sheets—Write-on transparencies
#753-621 (8½" x 11")

Oklahoma Embroidery Supply & Design
12101 I-35 Service Rd.
Oklahoma City, OK 73131
405-359-2741
www.embroideryonline.com
Backings, stabilizers, Isacord threads,
embroidery cards, and more

OttLight Technology
1214 W. Cass St.
Tampa, FL 33606
813-621-0058
True-color Ott Lights in floor, desk,
and clamp-on models

Pébéo of America, Inc.
PO Box 717
Swanton, VT 05488
819-829-5012
www.pebeo.com
Paints for glass, ceramics, and fabrics

The Picket Fence
www.appliquedesigns.com
Hemostats, patterns, and more

Provo Craft
285 E. 900 S.
Provo, UT 84606
800-937-7686
Glass ornaments and other crafts items

Sulky of America
3113 Broadpoint Dr.
Harbor Heights, FL 33983
www.sulky.com
Decorative threads (including Holoshimmer),
stabilizers, and bobbin threads

Superior Threads
PO Box 1672
St. George, UT 84771
435-652-1867
Email: RPurcell@infowest.com
Decorative threads and bobbin threads

Timid Thimble Creations
14298 Esprit Dr.
Westfield, IN 46074
317-818-9469
www.timidthimble.com
Quilter's Gloves by Nancy Odom

Walnut Hollow Farm, Inc.
1409 State Rd. 23
Dodgeville, WI 53533
800-950-5101
www.walnuthollow.com
Round wooden tray, plaque, and
other wooden crafts items

The Warm Company
954 E. Union St.
Seattle, WA 98122
206-320-9276
Warm & Natural batting and
Steam-A-Seam 2 fusible web

YLI Corporation
161 W. Main Street
Rock Hill, SC 29730
www.ylicorp.com
Decorative threads, ribbons, and bobbin threads

Sheila Haynes Rauen is an artist and designer who loves to work in a variety of mediums. Her fiber art allows experimentation with fabric, paint, stamps, beads, embroidery, and free-motion embroidery and quilting. She has been working with different arts and crafts manufacturers for several years, demonstrating a variety of techniques on television shows, such as the *Carol Duvall Show* and *Simply Quilts*. Sheila is the author of *Sassy Cats: Purr-fect Craft Projects* (Martingale & Company, 2000). She has also contributed to many magazines and the books *Creepy Crafty Halloween* (Martingale & Company, 2000) and *Hocus Pocus!* (Martingale & Company, 2003).

Sheila is a member of the Southern Highlands Craft Guild in Asheville, North Carolina; the Smoky Mountain Quilters; the Knoxville Arts and Cultural Alliance; and the American Quilter's Society. In addition to being an author and project designer, she designs fabrics for Clothworks, a division of FASCO/Fabric Sales, and is working on licensing her designs for use on other products as well. She and her husband live in Knoxville, Tennessee. They have two wonderful daughters, Haverly and Julie. Their cats, Natty and Gabriel, love to pose for Sheila in her studio as well as all around the house.

About the Author